Empowerment within (social) innovation

AF191959

To Nina and Arthur

Knut-Erland Berglund

EMPOWERMENT WITHIN (SOCIAL) INNOVATION

HOW INNOVATIVE ENTREPRENEURIAL ACTIVITY CAN ENSURE EQUALITY OF OPPORTUNITY

Korrekturläsning: Nina Zebergs & Knut-Erland Berglund

Förlag: BoD · Books on Demand, Östermalmstorg 1, 114 42
Stockholm, Sverige, bod@bod.se
Tryck: Libri Plureos GmbH, Friedensallee 273, 22763 Hamburg,
Tyskland

ISBN: 978-91-8080-876-7

Summary

Innovations arise in a context and are therefore characterized by norms and values. Research shows that markets favour technical product innovations in male-dominated companies and industries. To encourage a more equal situation, various initiatives, organizations and networks have been created, where methods have been developed to enable the development of innovation among those actors, industries and sectors stepmotherly treated in the field of innovation. This is to change the underlying system of norms and create greater prosperity through innovations.

Drawing on ideas of empowerment within social innovation, this study examines how organizations have developed innovative goods, services, methods, organizational forms, and social structures. The overall aim is to create understanding of innovation as a way of working to change the economy and societies.

The results show that the organizations studied have identified several *societal challenges and needs* of underrepresented groups in working life, business and regional development. They strive for *improvements* for individuals, organizations and society that increase gender equality in the aforementioned areas. They have developed several innovative *solutions* for increased gender equality in these areas. Their activities can thus be used as a starting point for defining the perspective of empowerment within social innovation as the development of new goods, services, methods and ways of organizing that are social in the sense that they identify and change hierarchical patterns in organizations and society. Based on a rhetorical analysis, the social innovation strategies have been presented and combined with previous research. The study's choice of method resulted in a *transferability* potential, that ideas and perspective can be used in other contexts due to a sense of nuance.

Preface

Since the 2000s, I have been interested in issues and topics related to social and political economy. It is about economics but also about the relationships that permeate different organizations, markets and societies. I wanted to show what underlying structures and what institutions or norms and values permeate a market economy.

I studied the situation of Dalits in the use of microcredit in the Hyderabad area of India. It turned out that through various interventions from microfinance, women could gain greater empowerment to participate in local politics and gain greater freedom of action within the family and extended family. My interest in political economy led me to later write a licentiate thesis (2013) on the sustainability and social responsibility of large Swedish companies. Corporate Social Responsibility (CSR) was current and fashionable during the same period. At first, CSR was somewhat stepmotherly cherished because various organizations and institutions considered it to be solely an Anglo-Saxon norm phenomenon. However, studies and my latest book showed that there are previous examples of corporate social responsibility also in Sweden and Scandinavia.

A continuation of my interest in social and political economy led me to social innovation. During the years 2013–2015, I was part of a research project at Luleå University of Technology that studied the topic of this book, namely what happens at the intersection of social innovation and gender and equality issues. This research project and the insights I gained there, resulted in this book.

This book examines the underlying norms regarding the area of innovation. What are the structures for innovation and what inclusive strategies can be used to get more women entrepreneurs noticed? Social innovation is related to other concepts and phenomena within social sustainable development, such as CSR and empowerment. I made other publications within the project together with researchers and with this book I try to give my perspective on the project through an empowerment approach.

Uppsala May 2025

Knut-Erland Berglund

Licentiate of Philosophy in Economic History,

Master of Philosophy in Economic History,

Bachelor of Philosophy in Geography

Table of Contents

I

II

Introduction: Empowerment within Social Innovation

"... prosperity on a national scale - mass flourishing - comes from broad involvement of people in the process of innovation".
Phelps (2013, p. vii)

In previous research and policy, innovation has primarily focused on technical product development in private companies, thereby overlooking many service industries, cultural and creative industries, the public sector and the idea-driven sector as a basis for developing innovative solutions to current and future needs (Lindberg, 2012; Moulaert et al. 2005; Pol & Ville 2009). However, there are opportunities to use the concept of social innovation to make socially, politically, creatively and culturally innovative processes visible (Moulaert et al. 2005). Phelps (2013) argues that if people at the grassroots level are given the space to act creatively based on their own needs, the conditions are created for a flourishing economy where curiosity and job satisfaction contribute to the development of innovations (social as well as technical). Innovations that, according to him, can help create the jobs of the future.

Furthermore, Phelps believes that if we are to live a "good life," we should create an economy and a society that rewards inclusion and innovation. To support his hypothesis, Phelps draws on Aristotle and Amartya Sen and argues that improvement, education, life choices and opportunities to express one's ideas are what we should strive for. A good life, in this context, is the opportunity to participate in and to create innovations on a broad front that improve both the individual, organizational and societal levels. According to Phelps, individuals gain more from creating and interacting with others than from consuming, although the latter is also an important part of the economy. Phelps shows that broader participation of people in innovation contexts existed in several Western countries during the period around 1830–1960, which, according to him, created jobs but also cultural phenomena such as music and literature.

In contrast to the innovation perspective that Phelps (2013) expresses above, different groups and perspectives have been downplayed in innovation research and innovation policy in recent decades. For example, women, the public sector and the idea-driven sector have often been overlooked, as it has mainly been technical product innovations and industries that have been recognized and promoted (Alsos et al. 2013; Andersson et al. 2012; Lindberg 2012; Lindberg & Schiffbänker 2013; Ranga & Etzkowitz 2010). In order to increase innovation research's opportunities to study inclusive innovation processes and thereby create a basis for stronger innovation development, this study documents and analyses a selection of the actors, industries and innovations that symbolize social innovation with an equal ambition. Inclusive innovation development refers here to innovation processes where a diversity of actors, groups, areas of activity, industries and sectors are involved in the identification of unmet social needs and in the development of innovative solutions to meet these needs (cf. Lindberg, 2014, 2015a). As part of this, a participatory research method is used where researchers and stakeholders together develop new relevant knowledge that can be translated into practical action to change prevailing exclusionary patterns in the field of innovation (cf. Aagaard Nielsen & Svensson 2006; Coghlan & Brydon-Miller 2014).

Social innovation, in the sense of the development of new goods, services, working methods, etc. that are social in their means and goals, constitutes a potentially rewarding entry point to inclusive innovation. This is because the concept encompasses the process of improving quality of life, well-being, relationships and empowerment at individual, organizational and societal levels (cf. Cajaiba-Santana 2014; Dawson & Daniel 2010; Moulaert et al. 2005). The intention is that the empowerment perspective will increase innovation research's opportunities to study inclusive innovation processes, where groups and perspectives that have so far been underrepresented or disadvantaged due to prevailing notions of sex/gender are involved in the development of new goods, services, working methods, etc. This was carried out with a joint knowledge development by three organizations - Winnet, Magma and Leia - that promote women's entrepreneurship and innovation. These have been selected because their activities exemplify how groups and perspectives can be practically involved in shaping the innovations of the future. The study shows how the concept of empowerment can make visible how these organizations have identified gender-related social needs of individuals, organizations and societies to develop innovative solutions to these needs in collaboration between different sectors of society.

Economically, culturally, politically and socially inclusive innovative processes can contribute to creating a large part of the prosperity in the Western world by allowing ideas to be developed, disseminated and implemented by many different actors in a variety of forms (Mokyr 2009; Phelps 2013; Törnqvist 2004). According to Phelps (2013), a large part of the current unemployment in Europe and other parts of the Western world is caused by the weakening of the innovative climate that historically founded prosperity. Recently, the European Union (EU) has highlighted social innovation to achieve inclusive societies and sustainable growth (European Commission 2013a). Social innovations are considered by the EU to contribute to processes that in themselves create products and services for profit and non-profit companies with new opportunities to increase and spread prosperity. The EU is investing, among other things, in research and promotion of innovative initiatives for the inclusion of marginalized groups such as the elderly, the poor, the unemployed, people on sick leave, and immigrants, to reduce exclusion and strengthen individuals' position in society. They are also investing in expanding the service sector in the Union, which they believe increases the need for social innovations (ibid).

Research on social innovation has become increasingly common in recent years, particularly in the USA, Canada, the UK and Germany (European Commission 2013a; 2013b). In Sweden, social innovation is also an established concept (Hansson et al. 2014; Lindberg & Berglund 2016; Nahnfeldt & Lindberg 2013). At the same time, the importance of social innovation is emphasized both in Sweden's national innovation strategy and in regional innovation strategies around the country (Ministry of Industry, Trade and Industry 2012). To understand how this kind of innovation develops, spreads and creates value in Sweden and to promote this in a conscious way, knowledge development is required in close collaboration with relevant societal actors. As stated at the beginning, democratic processes are assumed to be able to increase the well-being of people and the prosperity of nations (cf. Phelps 2013), while women, gender perspectives, the public sector and the idea-driven sector have largely been marginalized in research, policy and practice around innovation. This shows a normative skewed distribution of resources in society, which means that the potential for innovative development is lost. To harness this potential, it is necessary to make it clear that innovation is not only of a technical nature and that social innovation is not only valuable in itself for the development of individuals, organizations and society, but is also a prerequisite for technical innovations to be able to develop and create social value by fulfilling social needs and solving current societal challenges (Howaldt et al. 2015; Mulgan et al. 2007).

Previous research on gender and innovation has documented and analyzed gender-related patterns, where women, industries and sectors that employ the most women, women's organizations, and innovations in other forms than technical ones have been marginalized in previous policy and research (Alsos et al. 2013;

Andersson et al. 2012; Lindberg & Schiffbänker 2013; Pettersson 2007; Ranga & Etzkowitz 2010). Research on social innovation has created an understanding of people's needs and empowerment in innovation and social processes (Cajaiba-Santana 2014; Dawson & Daniel 2010; Evers & Ewert 2015; Howaldt et al. 2015). Connecting the areas of social innovation and gender and innovation increases the possibility of analyzing the process of social inclusion in the innovation area based on the power relations such as gender and sector that are focused on in this study (cf. Cajaiba-Santana 2014; Dawson & Daniel 2010; Moulaert et al. 2005). Since the ambition of the empowerment perspective is an increased understanding of how the inclusion of a diversity of actors, industries, sectors and innovations in the development of future goods, services and working methods can be achieved, this type of innovation is important to explore in order to increase insight into how the prevailing gender and sectoral relative marginalization in the field of innovation can change.

Purpose and questions

The purpose of the study is to study the possibilities and limitations of using ideas around empowerment within social innovation as a perspective for inclusive innovation. To achieve the purpose, three questions will be answered: 1) How is empowerment within social innovation expressed in the studied organizations? 2) How can participatory research approach help identify the opportunities and limitations of empowerment within social innovation? 3) How can previous research on social innovation and empowerment contribute to identifying the opportunities and limitations of the empowerment within social innovation perspective?

The study is based on joint knowledge development together with three organizations that promote women's entrepreneurship and innovation: Winnet, Magma and Leia. These all work with inclusive innovation processes that constitute valuable empirical evidence in the empowerment approach. Winnet Sweden is a non-profit umbrella organization for local and regional resource centers for women throughout Sweden with the aim of achieving gender-equal regional growth. Magma is a non-profit organization that brings together women in culture, equality and entrepreneurship in Sweden, Norway and Denmark with the aim of contributing to the professional and personal development of its members. Leia Företagshotell AB is a corporate hotel in Västerbotten that offers services for equal entrepreneurial development and an equal labour market.

The social innovation project and study

The study is based on the experience within the research project *Gendered social innovation - innovative ways to promote equal entrepreneurship/innovation,* which was run by Luleå University of Technology with funding from VINNOVA during 2013-2015. (See Lindberg & Karlberg 2015). The project aimed to increase knowledge about how Gendered social innovation is created and works in collaboration with three organizations that work to promote business and innovation: Winnet, Magma and Leia. The project has tested, analysed and developed knowledge about Gendered social innovation based on the organizations' operations. The problem identified in participating organizations and previous research studies is that Sweden's innovation and business promotion system, which has primarily been able to support the realization of business and innovation ideas in the form of technical product innovations among male-dominated companies and industries (Alsos et al. 2013; Lindberg et al. 2014; Lindberg & Johansson 2017; Pettersson 2007). The participating organizations have all developed methods for innovation and business promotion that can include a broader spectrum of actors, industries, sectors and innovations.

The experiences of the organizations studied are brought together in this study in a joint and systematic analysis of how a broader spectrum of actors can contribute to the innovation system at large. The analysis encompasses social innovation at the individual level (micro level), organizational level (meso level) and societal level (macro level) to capture the complexity of social innovation (cf. Cajaiba-Santana 2014; Dawson & Daniel 2010; Lindberg et al. 2015; Moulaert et al. 2005).

The study is based on a social innovation, participatory study and an empowerment approach. Together, the traditions enable a common, inclusive knowledge-building process, which both provides access to hard-to-reach data and enables contextually validating coordination with relevant stakeholders. The shared knowledge can also enable empowerment for the participants through increased understanding of themselves and the world around them, as well as increased scope for action (cf. Gunnarsson 2007, Gunnarsson & Westberg 2008; Herr & Andersson 2014).

Disposition
The introductory chapter has outlined theoretical and practical motivations for developing empowerment within social innovation as an inclusive way of studying the development of new goods, services, working methods, organizational methods and social structures. The next chapter describes the research fields of social innovation and empowerment perspectives. The method chapter explains how theoretical and practical knowledge has been developed. The next chapter contains the study's empirical data with descriptions of the three organizations' activities. The empirical evidence is then analysed to see the conditions for developing and discussing the possibilities and limitations of the proposed perspective.

Theory: Building the foundation for an Empowerment-within Social-Innovation-perspective

Introduction

The theory encompasses change processes at the individual level (micro level), organizational level (meso level) and societal level (macro level) to capture the complexity of the process of social inclusion that, according to previous research, characterizes socially innovative processes (cf. Cajaiba-Santana 2014; Dawson & Daniel 2010; Lindberg et al. 2015; Moulaert et al. 2005).

Phelps (2013) shows that in an innovative economy, both the number of jobs, the ability to collaborate, and the knowledge content of continuous problem solving change. According to him, creative work and the joy of creation at the micro level are the fundamental foundations of an innovative, inclusive economy at the macro level. According to him, innovation is based on ideas and an innovative economy creates space for a free flow of ideas as the basis for new products, services, working methods, etc. Important factors that, according to Phelps, make societies innovative are multiculturalism and multi-facedness at the macro level, where all kinds of people can create at the micro level. He believes that in such a society there are also many financiers at the meso level who can invest in promising ideas. According to Phelps, the heterogeneous expectations and identities of end users at the micro level are also important for the demand for new innovative solutions. There must also be interactivity and spontaneity in society for creative environments to be created, he believes, where everyday knowledge and specialist knowledge have the potential to meet across different borders. Meetings themselves are important, as meetings between different professions and people increase the plurality of knowledge conversations between them (cf. Bohlin 2009; Howaldt et al. 2015).

However, according to Phelps (2013), there are historical examples of social forms and political movements that have limited the possibility of inclusion, job satisfaction and innovation. According to him, the clearest examples can be found in the socialist-communist social model as well as the corporatist-fascist ditto (in Hitler's Germany and Mussolini's Italy). These are modern examples of economies and societies that reduced the innovative dynamics of their closed social systems through reduced economic freedom, restricted property rights and fewer financing opportunities. According to Phelps, the reduced dynamism can be seen in the significantly reduced degree of *grassroots innovation* developed by the community residents themselves *(indigenous innovation)*. In a top-down society, the opportunity and incentives to create, finance and access the resources required for inclusive innovation are reduced (Phelps 2007, 2013).

Social innovation

This section describes previous research on social innovation to study socially inclusive innovation processes. The basic definition of social innovation used in the study is the development of new solutions – in the form of new goods, services, methods, ways of organizing and social structures – that are social in their means and goals (cf. European Commission 2013a; Howaldt et al. 2015; Mulgan et al. 2007). 'Social' refers to quality of life, well-being, relationships and empowerment (Cajaiba-Santana 2014; Dawson & Daniel 2010; Pol & Ville 2009). By using social innovation as a theoretical lens, individual, organizational and societal renewal is made more visible than a one-sided technical understanding of innovation can (cf. Lindberg & Berg Jansson 2016).

Social innovation as a research area took off about 35 years ago within various social science disciplines but only gained a real boost in the last ten years. One of the first research areas to pay attention

17

to social innovation was urban planning. Social innovation developed as a critique of the dominant technological orientation in innovation policy and innovation research, where the focus was on improved competitiveness and organizational efficiency. However, Schumpeter had already discussed the necessity of social innovation in the 1930s, to facilitate technological innovation in society, although his focus was on the technical dimension of innovation (Moulaert et al. 2005).

Definitions of social innovation

Innovations have been described by some researchers as *embedded* in society's norms and systems, as their success depends on, for example, production systems, ideologies or cultural aspects (Howaldt et al. 2015). Traditionally, according to Howaldt et al., technological innovations have been seen as prerequisites for social change in the form of society's institutions (laws, norms and values), organizations and individuals changing their functioning/behavior *after* technological innovations have been established. They argue that this approach has ignored social and cultural dimensions of innovation. The social aspect of technological innovations and the technical elements of social innovations can be seen as intertwined and as a prerequisite for each other. According to them, Schumpeter anticipated the importance of the social aspect of innovations (although social innovations were marginal in his reasoning) and he noted that changes in the economy, culture and politics could form the basis for new technological innovations (ibid).

According to Godin (2012), it is important to distinguish the social dimension of innovation because innovation from the latter part of the 20th century was primarily associated with technical product development in companies. He believes that the narrow technical view of innovation makes other innovative contexts invisible, for example in civil society and the public sector. According to previous research, both social and technological innovations can contribute to addressing societal challenges and social needs, but the difference is that social innovation involves a conscious change in attitudes, behaviours and approaches in the establishment of new social practices (Cajaiba-Santana 2014).

Howaldt et al. (2015) define social innovation as follows:

"Social innovation is defined here as a new combination or configuration of practices in areas of social action, prompted by certain actors or constellations of actors with the ultimate goal of coping better with needs and problems that is possible by using existing practices" (p. 30).

Pol & Ville (2009) define social innovation as follows:

"... an innovation is termed social innovation if the implied new idea has the potential to improve either the quality or the quantity of life" (p. 881)

Dawson & Daniel (2010) define social innovation as follows:

"... social innovation... described as the development of new concepts, strategies and tools that support groups in achieving the objective of improved well-being" (p. 10).

Howaldt et al.'s (2015) definition is not as clear as this study's definition, as they are not explicit in what distinguishes social agency and social innovation. Social agency can also involve activities that are not innovative. Pol and Ville's and Dawson and Daniel's definitions focus on well-being, which is important but does not say everything about what a social innovation means. I have chosen to use this basic definition of social innovation: "the development of new solutions – in the form of new goods, services, methods, ways of organizing and social structures – that are social in their means and goals" (Lindberg et al. 2015; Mulgan et al. 2007). This is because it reflects the purpose and questions of the study by concretizing what social innovation is about at the micro, meso and macro levels.

Components of social innovation

Researchers have distinguished different components of social innovation. Cajaiba-Santana (2014), for example, outlines the social changes, improvements and well-being (e.g. 'empowerment') that characterize social innovation. Dawson and Daniel (2010) focus on people/individuals, the problem/opportunity, identifying problems, developing solutions, and improving people's quality of life, well-being, relationships, and empowerment. Lindberg and Berg Jansson (2016) draw attention to the identification of insufficiently addressed societal challenges and social needs, the involvement of affected groups in the development of solutions to these, the development and testing of these solutions with new social effects, and innovative collaboration between different groups, organizations and sectors. A central component of social innovation, according to previous research, is the movement from social exclusion to social inclusion (cf. Cajaiba-Santana 2014; Dawson & Daniel 2010; Moulaert et al. 2005).

In previous research, social innovation has been described in terms of new configurations of social practices that address social needs that have not been previously recognized or that meet such needs in a better way (Cajaiba-Santana 2014; Tjornbo 2015). Social innovations therefore do not have to be completely new in themselves but can be new combinations of existing components. Social innovations can also enable further innovation development, in both social and technical forms, by creating new collaborations and idea development (Mulgan et al. 2007).

Social innovation can be based on ideas about democracy, human rights, gender equality, etc. and, according to Evers and Ewerts (2015), strives for social improvement, which Mulgan et al. (2007) describes it as follows:

"(...) the development and implementation of new ideas (products, services and models) to meet social needs (...) aimed at the common good." (pp. 25-26).

The normative dimension in the understanding of social innovation means that the new social practices and structures should be "better" than the established ones (Mulgan et al. 2007). This means that a subjective assessment is made of what is considered better. Howaldt et al. (2015) argue that social innovations thus rarely reflect the values and needs of society as a whole but are only rooted in one or more groups of people. Changing and improving social practices and structures thus requires participants in the innovation process to reflect and analyze who and what will benefit from their activities. For example, organizations and systems such as the Ku Klux Klan and the Third Reich's concentration camps are questionable as social innovations from a democratic point of view, since they only improve society for a small group of people with a certain ideological conviction (ibid). It is therefore important to analyze the normative basis of each social innovation based on the specific societal context, with the understanding that general values can change over time (cf. McGowan & Westley 2015). In this study, such an analysis is made from an inclusive perspective, focusing on how actors, industries, sectors and forms of innovation that have previously been marginalized in innovation contexts can be made visible and involved.

Socially innovative inclusion

There is an ambition with social innovation to involve more people in the development of new goods, services, working methods, etc.

(Lindberg & Berglund 2016). Social innovation has thus been described in previous research as "inclusive" in the sense that it requires the participation of affected groups in civil society (Davies & Simon 2013), which is considered a prerequisite for *bottom-up* innovation by people at the grassroots level instead of *top-down* by already established experts (Lindberg 2014, 2015a). Affected groups such as users, consumers, residents, etc. are thus included in the development of new goods, services, working methods, etc. Social innovation processes are considered to be able to create free space and increased empowerment for groups that have been underrepresented in innovation development, including various groups of women (Lindberg et al. 2015; Lindberg & Berg Jansson 2016; Pettersson & Lindberg 2013).

Moulaert et al. (2005) show that civil society organizing has emerged in Europe from the grassroots level to create inclusion in various spheres of society such as the labor market, the education system, and other welfare areas. According to Moulaert et al., the recent boom in the social economy and self-help strategies (such as microfinance) are also expressions of locally innovative development. They believe that these movements criticize the legitimacy that the welfare society gives to certain already resource-rich groups, while other, more resource-poor groups are disadvantaged. To counteract such exclusion, according to Moulaert et al., social innovation is more about creating socially inclusive processes through multi-level *governance* and capacity building (for example, empowerment) than about ready-made solutions. Furthermore, they believe that groups that operate from the grassroots level are often the most innovative from a social perspective.

A socially innovative process can, according to Moulaert et al. (2005) give rise to new identities among those who have been marginalized in a way that increases their scope for action, while a greater focus on civil society's innovation development and the creation of new alternative institutions and processes can increase the empowerment of some groups at the expense of others. According to Moulaert et al., shared learning in innovation processes can increase both personal and collective empowerment (i.e. both at the micro and meso levels). Research shows that the development of social innovations often occurs through interaction between theory and practice, where both perspectives are considered important, where science is not considered to have ready-made answers to all questions, and where the answers emerge through interaction (Cipolla et al. 2015).

Disseminating social innovation

A central part of the understanding of social innovation is the possibility of spreading and using the developed solutions in contexts other than where they were developed, through so-called *contextual generalization* (cf. Czarnaiwska & Sevón 2005; European Commission 2013a; Mulgan et al. 2007). This is considered a prerequisite for social change at both the individual and organizational and societal levels (cf. Cajaiba-Santana 2014; Dawson & Daniel 2010; Moulaert et al. 2005). By constituting a kind of *quasi-concept* or *boundary object,* social innovation can link together similar phenomena in different geographical and social contexts (Lindberg & Portinson Hylander 2017; Star 1988). It creates a shared understanding of social innovation processes across organizational and sector boundaries, which facilitates the spread of social innovations (cf. European Commission 2013a).

Mulgan et al. (2007) argue that social innovation has difficulty developing and spreading where power is centralized, where communication is controlled and where there is no access to adapted resources. According to them, the conditions that instead favour social innovations are spontaneous meeting places, for example on buses, squares or digital forums. Historical examples are the coffee houses in 18th-century Vienna or 19th-century Glasgow where thoughts and ideas were developed and spread. What characterized these forums was, among other things, a "high ceiling" for ideas and practices (Hakelius 1995; Magnusson 2002). Many social innovations in the Western world came into being during the 19th century: kindergartens, self-help organizations, microcredit/savings banks, cooperatives, trade unions, model cities, etc. But the 1960s and 1970s also saw a wave of social upheaval that created many innovative ideas: ecology, feminism, human rights, labour law, etc. (cf. Berglund et al. 2016; Mulgan et al. 2007).

There may also be resistance to social innovations according to Mulgan et al. (2007). At first, people may be hostile to new solutions that force them to change their behaviours, they say. Some oppose new innovations because in the short term they increase transaction costs, that is, the cost of changing patterns of action, agreements, etc. Others, according to Mulgan et al., want stability because they have invested time and resources in the current order. Values and norms that permeate innovations can violate existing ones and can thus increase resistance among those who do not want to see change, they say. According to Mulgan et al., existing social networks can be limiting and conservative as they often favor already established relationships and innovations. One consequence of this is that incremental development is rewarded at the expense of more groundbreaking ideas. Even if an innovation has been introduced, according to Mulgan et al., it is not certain that it will be established.

Social innovation at micro, meso and macro levels

According to McGowan and Westley (2015), a social innovation can be understood as both a means and an end, which means that it can be both a process and a result of a process. Process then refers to the development of something new, often in collaboration between different actors (individuals, organizations, networks,

24

industries or sectors). The goal/result of such a process should improve people's quality of life, well-being, relationships and empowerment to be considered a social innovation. According to previous research, the result can be analysed based on three levels: 1) Meeting the social needs of underrepresented/disadvantaged groups (micro level/individual level), 2) Social changes in organizational structures (meso level/organizational level), 3) Social changes in societal structures (macro level/society level) (cf. Cajaiba-Santana 2014; Dawson & Daniel 2010; Lindberg & Berg Jansson 2016). At a more detailed level, social innovation can be distinguished in (at least) four forms (cf. Lindberg et al. 2015):

- New goods and services (micro level)
- New methods (micro level)
- New ways of organizing (meso level)
- New social structures (macro level)

The four forms of social innovation are interconnected and partly overlapping. An organization's dissemination of its socially innovative methods can lead to changed social structures. Socially innovative methods can also themselves facilitate the development of socially innovative goods and services. Innovative ways of organizing can be the result of innovative methods for collaboration across sector and organizational boundaries or the inclusion of marginalized groups, as in so-called *quadruple helix* constellations where authorities, universities, business and idea-based organizations collaborate in the development of innovations (cf. Carayannis & Campbell 2010; Jonsson 2014; Lindberg et al. 2012; 2014).[1]

---

[1]Historically, the non-profit organization methods that eventually led to the establishment of public welfare systems in Sweden can be seen as a social innovation process, where the welfare state changed the relationship between citizens and state (cf. Mulgan et al. 2007; Urban & mark 2010).

Howaldt et al. (2015) and Cajaiba-Santana (2014) complement each other in terms of understanding how social innovations are generated in an interaction between micro-, meso- and macro-levels. Creative imitation between individuals or between organizations has been highlighted as an important component of social innovation (cf. Howaldt et al. 2015; Johansson & Lindberg 2011). Howaldt et al. (2015) argue that macrostructures change through actions and events at the micro level, where people at the individual and organizational levels "mimic" each other and further develop each other's ideas. Dissemination thus becomes central to social innovation, where imitation starts a cultural learning process of creative further development. The spread of practices and ideas can shape the societal agenda, where political initiatives and institutions can thereby enable actors to question routines and patterns in order to change social practices and create new innovations, both social and technological. If this movement mechanism is supplemented with Cajaiba-Santana's (2014) structuring model where the micro, meso and macro levels are woven together, an understanding of what social innovation processes can look like is created (Fig. 1.1):

Fig 1.1 Model for the development of social innovations

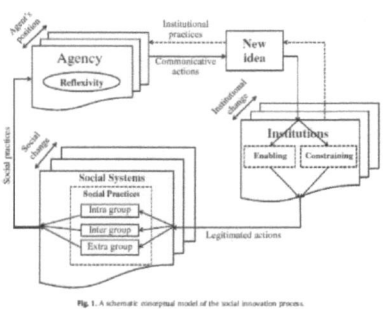

Source: Cajaiba-Santana (2014), p. 48.

26

The first level is represented by intra- *group innovation*, which is related to norms, values, rules, habits and conventions in a social group. The norms, values, rules and habits (institutions) that surround action at this level are group-related and require a micro-level analysis. At this level, it is important to understand the social and cognitive contexts that lead to either acceptance or rejection of new social practices. The role that individuals play here is an important part of the analysis in understanding the social interaction between individuals. The second level is represented by *intergroup innovation* where groups collaborate or compete in their relationships/networks based on different interests and power relations. Which group has influence over what is implemented or rejected is a central question here. The third level is represented by extra- *group innovation*, which is rarely investigated but deals with how social groups try to change their situation by advocating structural change at the macro level.

Criticism of social innovation

There has been some criticism of social innovation from various researchers. Among others, Dawson and Daniel (2010) have criticized the economization of social innovation by arguing that a social innovation must fundamentally be a process that aims to improve the social well-being of people and societies, rather than for direct commercial benefit (although this can be a side effect of the process). Another criticism has been made by researchers who see social innovation as a buzz word that has been used too loosely and ambiguously in research (Pol & Ville 2009). According to Pol and Ville, many studies focus either on the individual or structural level without connecting these with each other or with the meso level. This means that either the scope for action of individuals ("the heroic entrepreneur") or the power of structures is overemphasized and that an overly broad or too narrow definition of social innovation is used (Cajaiba-Santana 2014). To provide space for both the individual and structure, Cajaiba-Santana develops a structuring perspective with inspiration from, among other things, business ethics, strategy and management, organizational studies, etc. that connects an institutional perspective with agency:

"Through the interplay between institutions and actions, called the process of structuration, institutional practices shape human actions that, in turn, confirm or modify the institutional structure." (Cajaiba-Santana 2014, p. 47).

In this study, micro-, meso- and macro-levels are woven together to capture the complexity of the process from social exclusion to social inclusion that, according to previous research, characterizes social innovation (cf. Cajaiba-Santana 2014; Dawson & Daniel 2010; Lindberg et al. 2015; Moulaert et al. 2005).

Empowerment

As previously mentioned, innovation policy and innovation research in the Western world have primarily focused on technical product development in industrial companies, which has generally excluded other sectors, industries, actors and forms of innovation – especially those that involve many women (Alsos et al. 2013; Andersson et al. 2012; Lindberg & Schiffbänker 2013; Pettersson 2007). To increase inclusion, researchers, politicians and civil servants have advocated increased collaboration between different organizations and sectors in innovation development to create a multifaceted exchange of experiences and ideas. The need not to unilaterally support traditional actors in innovation contexts is considered important, as future innovations have the potential to come from many different organizations, networks and individuals (Lindberg 2014, 2015a; Lindberg et al. 2016).

The increased interest in social innovation in research and policy has meant that the importance of social processes for the generation of innovation has been emphasized in an increasing number of disciplines and areas of society. However, gender aspects have not been given the same attention to understand the complex contexts in which social innovations arise. According to some researchers, a gender analysis of social innovation can contribute to creating an understanding of how the distribution of power and resources affects the development of socially innovative solutions in different areas of activity. However, to date, there are only a few published scientific studies that interweave gender with social innovation (cf. Johnson Ross & Goddard 2015; Lindberg et al. 2015, 2016; Lindberg & Berglund 2016; Nahnfeldt & Lindberg, 2017).

To contribute to this emerging field of research, the study develops and deepens empowerment & social innovation. The ambition is to increase the possibilities for analysing inclusive innovation from a social innovation perspective. On a theoretical level, the study develops the research field of social innovation by identifying inclusion mechanisms at the individual, organizational and societal levels.

Empowerment over time
During the 19th century, a notion was established in many Western countries that women should take care of the home and that men should be entrepreneurs, managers, foremen and workers (Abrahamsson 2000). According to Du Rietz (2013), entrepreneurship among women from the 18th century until the 1920s was much greater than in later periods, when women were primarily housewives and after 1970 women were primarily employed. This within the Swedish economy and society. Women made up roughly the same proportion of entrepreneurs as men during the 18th and 19th centuries. After the abolition of the guild system and the introduction of freedom of trade, trade in the cities expanded and it became easier to establish oneself as a self-employed person. With increasing trade union influence and general

concern about worker protection, during the late 19th century and early 20th century, legislation banning overtime and night work affected small business owners in general and women in particular. There was also an idea within social democracy and the labour movement to create large-scale industrial production where small businesses would be replaced by large companies, which affected women's entrepreneurship.

Du Rietz (2013) sees three main reasons for women's decline in entrepreneurship. The first was the planned economy (1932) which would ensure that companies were slowly nationalized. During the 1940s, this effort was intensified with the Rehn-Meidner model, which through wage policy would ensure that "inefficient" companies would close and the workforce would be transferred to expanding sectors. This had consequences for smaller service and craft businesses, which were seen as low-productive, which disappeared, especially in the textile industry (which was a female-dominated industry). The second was the additional labor legislation during the 1970s that affected the economic opportunities of smaller companies. The third reason for women's decreased entrepreneurship was the greater influence of municipalities, which during the 20th century came to incorporate preschools and daycare centres, due to the collectivism and large-scale nature of society. Women went from being self-employed to housewives (1950s) and to dominating the jobs that have been created in the public sector since the 1970s.

Women were thus more active as entrepreneurs during the 18th and 19th centuries than during the latter part of the 20th century in Sweden. Since women throughout history have not always had equal opportunities for entrepreneurship, they were forced to organize themselves as non-profits to improve their situation, according to Du Rietz (2013). Since the 19th century, women have been involved in non-profit associations that could pave the way for women's independent professional ambitions and livelihood opportunities. These associations were based on non-profit work that, as they expanded, employed paid staff, including childcare activities for working mothers. This discussion shows how the historical development of the social structures of the labour market and business sector has affected the scope for action for women and men to make a living and realize their ideas. This is relevant in order to be able to analyse in this study how the studied organizations' ability to change social exclusion to social inclusion in innovation.

Empowerment and social relationships

Previous research on empowerment can contribute to understanding how power in terms of status, resources and scope for action is distributed between women and men in organizations and society (cf. Kabeer 2003; Nussbaum 2011; Sen 1999). Empowerment is used in this study to analyze whether and how the activities of the organizations studied have increased the scope for action for marginalized groups in the development of new goods, services, working methods, etc. Empowerment is about which action alternatives and abilities an individual has access to. Eduards (2002) emphasizes the understanding of women's agency as important for the distribution of power in society, inspired by Amartya Sen, who has specialized in how human capabilities relate to economic development. Amundsdotter (2010) has also, inspired by Sen, emphasized that human rights and power are linked to individuals' well-being. To examine and analyse people's possibilities for action (and thus to live the life they want), the following dimensions of empowerment can be noted: capabilities, agency, resources and achievements (cf. Kabeer 2003; Nussbaum 2011; Sen 1999).

According to Nussbaum (2011) and Sen (1999), abilities are first and foremost individual and only indirectly collective. Kabeer (2003) and Nussbaum (2011) have shown central abilities for people to live dignified lives. These include human rights such as freedom of assembly, freedom of political opinion, private property (both immovable and movable), property rights on the same terms as others, the right to seek employment on the same terms as others, to be free from search and detention on unjustified grounds, to be assigned humane tasks in working life, the right to exercise practical reason and have meaningful, mutually recognisable relationships, and to be both economically and politically competent.

Zohir and Matin (2004) have operationalized human rights as economic, social, political, and cultural aspects of human capabilities. Economic aspects include inequality, poverty, infrastructure, new institutions and businesses, sustainability, and inclusion in working life and business. Education, health and the like can also be included in both economic and social aspects. Social aspects also include social capital, power relations (based on gender, ethnicity, age, etc.) and demographics. Political aspects include being able to stand in democratic elections, having relationships with authorities, political mobilization and policy influence, and exercising democratic rights. Cultural aspects include, for example, gender relations and religion. If these four aspects of empowerment transition from individual abilities to more structural states, it could mean increased scope for action for many people (Berglund 2007; Zohir & Matin 2004).

To further define empowerment, one can distinguish what constitutes a reduction in empowerment, so-called *disempowerment* (Nussbaum 2011). For example, education generally leads to the development of people's abilities, but a political process that does not include citizens reduces their opportunities to influence society and their own lives (cf. Nussbaum 2011). This example highlights that strengthening people's abilities is not automatically emancipatory but requires a truly inclusive process.

Two gender science approaches used in this study to understand gender patterns in the field of innovation are *doing gender* and *undoing gender* (cf. Acker 1999; Deutsch 2007). Doing gender is a scientific concept that enables analyses of gender as an ongoing process of interaction between people through which gender-based categories are created, maintained and changed (Abrahamsson 2000; Acker 1999; West & Zimmermann 1987). This everyday practice of gender can contribute to either changing or maintaining prevailing gender patterns. Often, however, existing structures are tenacious and resistance to change is often strong, as illustrated in the following quote:

"The resistance reveals that there are power relations involved, requiring negotiations about 'what men and women are allowed to do, how they are allowed to behave and how men and women are to be ranked and valued'" (Kvande 2003, pp. 37-38).

Undoing gender involves a loosening of prevailing gender patterns so that the segregation and hierarchy between women and men, femininity and masculinity, are erased (Deutsch 2007). To achieve this, it is necessary to make differences in power, status and resources between men and women visible, which gender research contributes to (Lindberg & Schiffbänker 2013).

An everyday perspective

Innovation[2], has come to be seen as a solution to many countries' economic challenges in maintaining and increasing growth and welfare (Alsos et al. 2013; Andersson et al. 2012). Among other things, both the EU and Sweden invest extensive public funds in innovation development (Lindberg & Schiffbänker 2013; Mulgan et al. 2007). However, these investments have mainly included

---

[2]in the sense of developing new goods, services, working methods, etc. that are beneficial to society.

technical product development in private companies in male-dominated industries, which has limited the view of what innovation is (Lindberg 2012; Pettersson 2007). This has contributed to making invisible the innovation that takes place in the public sector (including healthcare, schools, social care), private service industries (including hospitality, cultural and creative industries) where most women are active as employees or entrepreneurs, and in idea-based activities (including social inclusion in working and social life) where several women's organizations are active. Women's innovation development has thus been marginalized in innovation policy and research. The technical view of innovation entails a gender-based exclusion in the field of innovation, which has been analyzed in previous research from various gender science perspectives (cf. Alsos and others 2013; Andersson et al. 2012; Lindberg & Schiffbänker 2013).

As part of understanding, paying attention to and changing which actors are given space in society when it comes to innovation, Lie and Sörensen (1996) suggest that the concept of innovation can be democratized by making visible the importance of the social and local context for the development and benefit of innovations. They emphasize the value of "everyday knowledge" because, according to them, innovations require anchoring in people's everyday lives to become meaningful and useful. Democratization of innovation thus includes making innovative adaptation visible in people's everyday lives. In previous research, as previously mentioned, innovation processes are often described as something extraordinary, even though creativity is often rooted in people's everyday lives, which means that innovation can still be described as creative imitation (cf. Alsos and others 2013; Howaldt et al. 2015; Johansson & Lindberg 2011; Lindberg et al. 2014).

In the innovation model that, Swedish authorities often use to promote innovations, *the Triple Helix*, the interaction between business, government and academia is seen as central to the pace of innovation in the economy (Lindberg 2014, 2015a). However, both women and the idea-based sector are marginalized in this model because small businesses that women often run are seen as irrelevant, as are the non-profit organizations that work to promote women's entrepreneurship and innovation (Lindberg et al. 2012, 2014). As a more inclusive innovation model, *the quadruple helix* has therefore been launched, which also includes smaller companies and the idea-driven sector, which is a model that has been developed in parallel by various research groups over the past decade (cf. Carayannis & Campbell 2010; Jonsson 2014; Lindberg et al. 2012, 2014). There, marginalized groups are given more academic and government resources to improve opportunities for innovation among a diversity of actors, sectors and industries. As a small business owner, it is often difficult to get in touch with authorities and universities to gain access to resources and knowledge (Lindberg et al. 2014). Alsos and others (2013) argue that innovation research can become more inclusive through increased understanding of how innovations develop in practice, which can be achieved by analyzing the context in which innovations arise, and which actors have been involved in shaping them, which *the quadruple helix* model enables (cf. Lindberg et al. 2012, 2014).

Method: Individual and collective learning

Introduction

To create transparency and self-reflection in the study, in this chapter I discuss the focus of the study, how the organizations have been studied, my learning process and how together we have been able to develop new practical and theoretical knowledge. This includes a critical reflection on the view of science, the view of knowledge, the view of humanity and the view of democracy (cf. Anderson 2012).

Study participation orientation

Action research saw the light of dawn during the 1940s in the USA, where social psychologist Kurt Lewin created a research tradition that would assist practitioners with locally rooted knowledge (Herr & Anderson 2014; Johansson 2008). *Action research* and *organizational development/learning* are approaches that come from Lewin and constitute research-based problem solving in everyday life situations. These studies examined production and working conditions in factories and discrimination against minority groups. This was a criticism of Taylorism, which Lewin believed manipulated workers into increasing productivity. The research tradition that Lewin initiated has changed over time and has become increasingly linguistically focused in the spirit of Wittgenstein and Habermas. Since the 1940s, several directions have broadened action research, which has thereby increasingly come to be called *participatory* research, which is the term I have chosen to use in my study (Aagaard Nielsen & Svensson 2006; Coghlan & Brydon-Miller 2014; Johannisson et al. 2008; Svensson et al. 2002b). Some examples of orientations that are particularly relevant to my study are discussed below.

Three common denominators in participatory research are: 1) That different types of knowledge are integrated into knowledge development, 2) The effort to create equal cooperation between researchers and those affected, 3) That research should explicitly contribute to practical change processes (Lindberg 2010; Winther Jörgensen 2008). What distinguishes different approaches within participatory research is, among other things, whether they belong to the pragmatic or critical tradition (Johansson & Lindhult 2008). In the pragmatic tradition, interpretation and action are not distinguished and change processes focus on workplaces (within a group). Consensus and practical action are valued more highly than theoretical development within this tradition. The pragmatic tradition stems from Lewin and the focus on *organizational development/learning*. In the critical tradition, critical thinking and reflection are considered to precede practical action. Action and dialogue are then seen as two interconnected but distinct elements. To provide tools for change, where one attempts to change societal norms through a diversity of perspectives (Herr & Anderson 2014; Johansson & Lindhult 2008; Lindberg 2010). In light of these orientations, my study is characterized by *a participatory perspective, joint research initiation, empowerment, theoretical and practical knowledge development through abduction.*

A critical tradition and participatory research

The study can be considered to have emerged from the participatory tradition because joint seminars with researchers and practitioners where a diversity of voices and innovation development have been given space have been a springboard for the development of knowledge and action. Action and reflection have thereby built on each other while constituting two different activities (cf. Johansson & Lindhult 2008). In participatory research, such inclusion has been justified by the fact that it gives rise to more *socially robust knowledge* where the conclusions are regularly checked with the actors operating in the practical context. Including more actors and perspectives unites participation and empowerment perspectives as the perspectives of certain groups have historically often been overlooked. (Gunnarsson 2007; Gunnarsson & Westberg 2006, 2008). The participating organizations in the project – Winnet, Magma and Leia – are all working to change norms in innovation development, which has been used in the joint knowledge development to further develop existing innovation research and increase their scope and empowerment to promote innovation in a more inclusive way. In this way, participation perspectives and *empowerment* aspects are combined in the study.

Joint research initiation and empowerment

My project was initiated by both researchers and participating organizations in line with a participatory research tradition (cf. Aagaard Nielsen & Svensson 2006; Coghlan & Brydon-Miller 2014; Svensson et al. 2002b). The roles that researchers and organizations took on in the project are similar to those described in *interactive research* , which is the name for a Nordic variant of participatory research where the role of researchers is to research *with* , rather than *to* or *for* , stakeholders, who in turn become co-researchers in a joint knowledge-developing process (Aagaard Nielsen & Svensson 2006; Johannisson et al. 2008). The view of practitioners as co-researchers is also found within the participatory approach of *practice-driven theory* . The interactive research then becomes a learning process rather than a creator of ready-made answers or solutions, which can contribute to increased understanding among the participants of their own situation in the organization or society (Docherty et al. 2008).

Empowerment (and emancipation) means, according to Freire, that participants in an interactive research process gain increased insight into their situation within an organization or society at large, which can increase their scope for action to change the situation based on their needs (Andersson 2012; Svensson et al. 2002).

Stakeholders are seen in the study as important co-researchers based on their experiences and knowledge of their own situation. As co-researchers, they contribute to creating a shared meaning in the theme being studied. In this spirit, the concept of *conscientization* was established by Freire, who draws attention to how social, political or economic contradictions between groups can be bridged, where marginalized groups are given tools to strengthen their own role in society (Berglund & Danilda 2008). In line with this, the project has aimed to increase the empowerment of the participating organizations through joint knowledge-building.

Theoretical and practical knowledge development through abduction

Participatory research is based on communication and n communicative contexts, language confusion can easily occur, as statements can be misunderstood, misinterpreted, etc. Power relations also permeate communication, even though participatory research in the spirit of Habermas strives for free and equal communication between participating parties (Herr & Anderson 2014). The project's participatory knowledge development can be seen as a kind of research circle[3] in the sense that the participating organizations, together with the project's researchers, have studied their own activities through continuous dialogue (cf. Holmstrand 2008). Like the participatory approaches *participatory research* and *participatory evaluation,* the research circle as a method is associated with Freire, who criticized the prominent role that conservative, white men's theoretical models have played in action research. Freire's research also attempts to challenge the dualistic views of the positivist traditions, which can be seen in the following

---

[3]A research circle is a study circle that researchers and fellow researchers participate in. Historically, study circles come from the labour movement. Research circles as a method have been developed in close collaboration between research and working life (Andersson 2012; Holmstrand 2008).

examples: theory/practice, subject/object, macro/micro (Herr & Anderson 2014). The goal of participatory research is, according to Wingblad and Jonsson (2008, pp. 311-312) "... to generate new knowledge that is practically useful and also theoretically interesting". In the project, the participants' experiences, perspectives and forms of knowledge have been intertwined with knowledge from previous research in empowerment and innovation, and social innovation, respectively, to create new knowledge about innovation. Thereby, an abductive approach has been applied in the study process, that is, an interaction between induction[4] and deduction[5]. Questions and conclusions have then been continuously adjusted in dialogue between researchers and participants, which is consistent with the participatory approach *of interactive critical research* where affected actors reconsider their beliefs to innovatively change their patterns of action, which creates a kind of *rhizomatic validity* (cf. Lindberg 2010). Such a reassessment takes place through communication, dialogue and inclusion of participants' different voices (Berglund & Danilda 2008).

There are also similarities between the project's focus and the participatory focus of *practice-driven theory,* where researchers and stakeholders jointly reflect on problem formulations and analyses to generate new practically relevant but also theoretically interesting knowledge. This knowledge is based to some extent on the *tacit knowledge* (or familiarity knowledge) that participants possess based on their experiences of the current context (Bohlin 2009; Wingblad & Jonsson 2008). Heidegger (in Furberg 2005) and Habermas (1996) speak of a kind of "craftsmanship", where understanding is created by putting on someone else's tools of knowledge.

---

[4]Induction = Based on empirical observations and results, new theory is generated (Bryman 2002).
[5]Deduction = Based on existing theories, the researcher formulates hypotheses that are tested against empirical evidence (Bryman 2002).

Davis (1999) shows the importance of the reflexive work of creating new questions and testing these against experiences to once again ask new questions of the "material" that is being qualitatively worked with. This reflexivity does not get stuck in the dichotomy between theory and practice but instead focuses on what unites them. In the project, such a pendulum movement has been created in the meeting between different experiences, perspectives and forms of knowledge within the framework of the dialogues between researchers and fellow researchers conducted at the project's seminars, which are described later in this chapter. The seminars have constituted a kind of *free space* where participants have been able to test different forms of knowledge and contextualize them (cf. Lindberg 2010; Schwencke 2006). This has also created *transferability* in the sense that generalized knowledge has been shaped and *reshaped* based on the local context (cf. Herr & Anderson 2014). At the seminars, a bridge between theory and practice has been created, where both propositional knowledge and skills knowledge have been used in the development of knowledge. The contextualized knowledge created by the participants has contributed to making the knowledge simultaneously local and general, that is, the knowledge produced is valid both in a certain context and can be theorized so that it becomes general (cf. Merton 2012).

Working abductively is an advantage in participatory research because such processes inevitably involve both inductive and deductive processes. The social systems that are the focus of participatory research are constantly changing because people think and act in new ways, which means that *grand theories* – that is, theories that claim to unambiguously explain behaviours and phenomena – are poorly suited to participatory research (Chalmers 2005; Wingblad & Jonsson 2008). The change in society's forms of knowledge can be seen in the fact that the industrial society has now been supplemented by an information society and a service society, where more actors than universities create and disseminate scientific knowledge (Nowotny et al. 2001). The contextual knowledge developed through participatory research can be transferred and reinterpreted in other contexts via so-called *reflective communities (communities of inquiry)* (Svensson et al. 2002a).

Process structure, roles and validity

This section describes how the empirical data collection was carried out and which activities for joint knowledge development have been carried out. In addition, the roles that researchers and participants have had in the process are discussed, as well as how the pendulum movement between proximity and distance that characterizes participatory research has been handled. Finally, it is discussed which validity criteria are relevant for assessing the quality of the process and results of participatory research.

Empirical collection and analysis

In the project, the knowledge arena around empowerment and social innovation has been expanded through the organizations' active participation in the research process' problem formulation, material collection, analysis and dissemination. The joint problem formulation, which has similarities with the participatory method of reflective community, began even before the project was formulated, during several years of dialogue between the university and the organizations regarding the innovation area's gender-related prioritization patterns. When the state agency VINNOVA announced funding for research and development projects on needs-based research for increased gender equality, Luleå University of Technology applied for funding in collaboration with Winnet, Magma and Leia, which was granted.

The joint knowledge development in the project was organized in three phases:

Autumn 2013 – Exchange of experience on methods for Gendered social innovation
1) Seminar with participating researchers and organizations for joint empirical collection on the organizations' activities
2) Empirical collection through self-studies in organizations

Spring and autumn 2014 – Development of the concept of Gendered social innovation
1) Seminar with participating researchers and organizations for joint analysis of the empirical material
2) Joint analysis by researchers and participating organizations through continuous reconciliation of texts

Spring and autumn 2015 – Dissemination of methods for Gendered social innovation
1) Seminar with participating researchers and organizations for joint planning of dissemination and use of the project's results
2) Joint formulation of a popular science orientation book on Gendered social innovation
3) National conference for the dissemination of knowledge and methods for Gendered social innovation
4) Dissemination of results on Gendered social innovation through, among other things, scientific articles

The empirical collection was carried out in two different ways: 1) seminar rooms for joint empirical collection (which were recorded and transcribed and documented through notes), 2) *self-studies* (where the organizations themselves formulated descriptions of their activities in writing, which were then further developed in dialogue between the researchers and the organizations). The material presented in the empirical chapter of the study thus consists partly of quotes and notes from the seminars, and partly of a joint further development of the organizations' texts.

The analysis was carried out in three different ways: 1) seminar for joint knowledge development where the collected empirical material was analysed jointly by the researchers and the organizations (which was documented through notes), 2) writing of a popular science orientation book, scientific articles based on the joint analysis, carried out by the researchers in dialogue with the organizations, 3) continuous coordination where the researchers and the organizations read and commented on each other's texts with description and analysis. The analyses that I have formulated in this study are therefore based on an interweaving of my own thoughts, those of other researchers and organizations in accordance with a participatory research method (cf. Aagaard Nielsen & Svensson 2006; Coghlan & Brydon-Miller 2014; Johannisson et al. 2008; Svensson et al. 2002b).

Each seminar lasted 3-5 hours, with 1-2 representatives from each organization participating in addition to 3-4 researchers from the project. Both researchers and organizations actively participated in knowledge generation at the seminars and contributed their different experiences, perspectives and forms of knowledge. The researchers contributed knowledge from previous research on gender and innovation and social innovation as a basis for joint discussions about the organizations' experiences. The organizations contributed experiences from their practical efforts to promote women's entrepreneurship and innovation. At the seminars, a joint analysis was carried out of how the organizations' activities could be understood based on the definitions of social innovation presented in previous research, as a starting point for a discussion about what Gendered social innovation encompasses and means.

The seminars have constituted a kind of free space where participants were able to express their opinions separate from their everyday contexts. This free space was characterized by "high ceilings" so that the participants could reflect on their everyday lives from a visionary horizon. (cf. Lindberg 2010; Schwencke 2006). The seminars are also related to the participatory *research circle* method, where researchers and stakeholders jointly develop new knowledge in democratic knowledge processes. Research circles are based on the common themes or problems that the participants identify and should lead to increased knowledge about these that can be used by the participants in practical action (Andersson 2010; Holmstrand 2008; Lindberg 2010).

To increase reflexivity in the research process, in addition to my notes from the seminars, I have also kept notes in a diary to document my experiences of both the seminars and other elements of the project. However, this has not been done as diligently as prescribed in the participatory method, *a chronicle of research decisions*, where the researcher documents their choices and actions and the consequences they have had. In such a case, the researcher's thoughts, feelings and expression can become more visible than otherwise (Lindberg 2010). In the diary, I wrote down the following, among other things: in-depth questions to ask the organizations, methodological reflections from, for example, anthropology on how access to an empirical field can be created, previously read literature that can be related to the project, and reflections on the dissemination of knowledge.

The combination of the different approaches for empirical collection, analysis and reflection means that relevant aspects have been continuously explored individually and collectively in accordance with a *cyclical learning process* where several different actors participate in a pendulum movement between theory and practice (cf. Svensson et al. 2002a). In this way, qualitative and

45

contextualized knowledge has been created based on both formal and informal knowledge (so-called familiarity knowledge or tacit knowledge). This is because the process, in addition to knowledge of statements, has been able to value practical knowledge (cf. Bohlin 2009). This can be compared to the participatory research method *knowledge workshop*, where the participants' tacit knowledge is made visible to understand the studied theme in a multifaceted way (Lindholm 2002). Bohlin (2009) believes that tacit knowledge is a form of experience-based knowledge that cannot be fully conveyed through language but through performance. I feel that the silent experience of implementing the project's participatory process has become a key to understanding the assertion knowledge from previous research that constitutes the theoretical frame of reference in my study.

Roles in the process

By working with participatory research, where voices from outside the university are included, I distance myself from the traditional *desk researcher* who, in his or her professional practice, is distanced from the practice he or she studies, in both a physical, mental and social sense (cf. Johannisson et al. 2008; Olsson 2002). Instead, I have taken on the role *of familiarity researcher* in the participatory process. By not objectifying, that is, not unilaterally attributing characteristics to, the people included in the study and instead encouraging communication, reflection and self-understanding among both researchers and participants, the role of the familiarity researcher leads to individuals being made aware of their situation and thus given tools for action (cf. Wingblad & Jonsson 2008). Such *a co-creative researcher role* creates the conditions for underrepresented and disadvantaged groups to participate in scientific knowledge development in a way that can contribute to increasing these groups' scope for action (Johansson 2008; Lindberg 2010).

One advantage of participatory research is gaining access to an empirical field and its affected groups in a way that would otherwise be difficult. Involving affected groups in the research process increases the likelihood that empirical collection and analysis will be reliable, which is discussed in more detail later in this section. The collection and compilation of the project's empirical data has been partly carried out by the participating organizations themselves, who have thereby studied their own practice in accordance with the participatory research method self-studies (cf. Lindberg 2010). One risk with this is that participants are eager to deliver information that they themselves consider to be most beneficial to themselves. This was handled by comparing the organizations' statements with each other and with previous research at the seminars (cf. Bryman 2002; Herr & Anderson 2014).

My role in the project has been open in the sense that all participants knew that my background and that I had the assignment to document what was said at the seminars, where I was also involved in the discussions. The advantage of having an open role is that ethical problems are reduced. I did not have to resort to the deceptions of the hidden role, which means that participants cannot consent to participate and that their right to privacy is violated (cf. Bryman 2002). I became both an *insider* and *an outsider* in the project. I was an outsider because as an outsider I had to familiarize myself with Winnet, Magma and Leia's operations. I was an insider regarding seminar culture from my previous studies at undergraduate and postgraduate level because I knew what values should permeate a seminar, that is, to be an active participant, to listen and to contribute to the joint discussion (cf. Habermas 1996; Herr & Anderson 2014).

My learning process
During my undergraduate education in economic history, I investigated the globalization tendencies of markets, the influence

of elites over the Swedish ironmongering trade in the 18th century, and the impact of microfinance on the *empowerment* of the poorest and most vulnerable group in India, namely Dalit women (Berglund 2007). Microfinance is a way of developing society from the bottom up, as pointed out by the Nobel Committee (2006) when Muhammad Yunus – founder of the microcredit concept Grameen Bank in Bangladesh – received the Nobel Peace Prize. In 2008, I had the opportunity to write a licentiate thesis in economic history at Uppsala University. Because my interest in the subject was in line with economists and philosophers such as Amartya Sen and Martha C. Nussbaum, I became interested in the ethics and social responsibility of (large) companies, or *Corporate Social Responsibility* (CSR) as it has come to be called. In contrast to the bottom-up approach that often characterizes social innovation, the CSR work of influential actors such as large corporations can be seen as a top-down approach. for social development. In my licentiate thesis (Berglund 2013) I analysed the rhetorical content of large Swedish companies' CSR and sustainability reports (cf. Schwartz & Carroll 2003).

After my Licentiate of Philosophy degree, I was employed in 2013 in a research project at Luleå University of Technology. The project aimed to document and analyse Gendered social innovation in the organizations Winnet, Magma and Leia, which all work to promote women's entrepreneurship and innovation. During the process, I have come to realize that my undergraduate education in studies of women's conditions and my licentiate thesis in economic history with a focus on CSR constitute important pieces of the puzzle for understanding innovation from an inclusive perspective. I saw a similarity between corporate CSR work and social innovation because both create platforms for dialogue, shared learning, and collaboration. In CSR terms, companies are interested in identifying and involving various *stakeholders* and bringing together relevant actors for an exchange of ideas and practices in the development of new solutions to create positive social impacts from the companies' operations. Similarly, social innovation is about creating platforms to involve affected people in social development processes.

Proximity and distance

Proximity is presented as desirable in participatory research and requires a critical distance from the material. (Bryman 2002; Herr & Anderson 2014). *Going native* is seen by anthropologists as a problem where the researcher risks unthinkingly adopting the worldview of those studied. Johannisson (2008) argues that instead of seeing going native as a threat, it should be seen as an opportunity for insight through deep personal engagement. The proximity then contributes to increased understanding of the nature of the theme being studied. Gunnarsson and Westberg (2008, p. 264) argue that participatory research also requires a multifaceted view of the discourses that occur in the contexts of which one becomes a part as a participating researcher:

"It is important as a researcher not to be seduced by the discourses but also *to go behind the discourses* and see what lies in the shadow of the dominant discourses" (*my emphasis*).

What I think both Gunnarsson, Westberg and Johannisson show is that participatory research is based on a critically reflective closeness to the subject and the participants, instead of having a distanced relationship to the "object of study" of the practice in a positivist manner.[6] Instead, adopting an openness towards the participants and the context is the key to participatory research, as contextual validity can then be increased (Lindhult 2008). Joint knowledge development can increase the validity of research by making visible what are adequate questions and conclusions in the specific context. Thus, concerns that going native would be a

---

[6]However, Gunnarsson & Westberg (2008) have an important dividing line where they emphasize distance through the study of underlying/underlying causes of a situation, which in this study is handled using rhetorical methods.

problem for the validity of research should instead be seen as a way that leads to new questions and actions by testing knowledge in practice. For example, by allowing different forms of knowledge (theoretical, practical and tacit knowledge) to come together, the participants in the process can create *correspondence validity* , that is, a correspondence with the participants' composite experiences and understandings.[7] When project participants and researchers have read and revised each other's texts, this is a form of *discursive validation* that can help meet *the criterion of congruence* . If this process is documented, one can also achieve *transparency* or auditability of the research (cf. Lindberg 2010; Lindhult 2008).

Since the joint seminars for knowledge development with the studied organizations were limited in time and space, a distance was also made possible where I as a researcher could withdraw and reflect on the process from different theoretical perspectives. In participatory research, the researcher is in this way both a practitioner and a theorist, that is, a *reflective practitioner* (Johannisson 2008). Both we researchers and the participating organizations underwent a learning process in the process (Herr & Anderson 2014, p. 69).

Analysis method

To analyse the study's empirical material, I use so-called *rhetorical methods* (cf. Foss 2009; Hill 2009) which makes it possible to identify and analyse underlying structures and strategies in the studied context (cf. Gunnarsson & Westberg 2008). Sorting and analysis of the empirical evidence based on rhetorical methods was done in collaboration with the organizations studied to ensure a social contextualization of the interpretations (cf. Merton 2012). The sorting and analysis were first carried out using a rhetorical

---

[7] It is important to emphasize that the process primarily involved researching "with" rather than "for" or "at" the participating organizations, given the go-native issue.

clustering method (cf. Foss 2009) to distinguish claims and activities in the studied organizations that can be related to the process from social exclusion to social inclusion that, according to previous research, is central to social innovation (cf. Cajaiba-Santana 2014; Dawson & Daniel 2010; Moulaert et al. 2005). The cluster method offers a critical and structured way of approaching the key areas and concepts that permeate a text (Foss 2009). It makes it possible to circle the keywords that a text consists of. These words do not have to be spoken per se, but can be an interpreted spiritual meaning of the written word. The words and concepts covered by the key concepts constitute so-called "clusters" (ibid).

The cluster method was complemented by the rhetorical gender method because the purpose of this study is to analyze inclusion and exclusion in innovations, which is made possible by the gender perspective (Nudd & Whalen 2009). The rhetorical gender method in this study is based on the categories of *redefining, recovering* and *revising* . Gender studies research on rhetoric has previously used these three concepts to analyze rhetorical artifacts such as descriptions of organizations (ibid). According to Nudd and Whalen (2009), *reformulation* is about creating a language that makes visible and problematizes society's perceptions of women and men by showing the masculine norms that create social differences between these categories. This is done by creating new contexts and new social platforms for interpretation and language use. According to them, language shapes the ideas and concepts that organizations use to design their operations. *Reclaiming* is about highlighting marginalized women's creation of new meanings and innovations. For example, women have been marginalized as writers, politicians, and innovators. *New visions* are about creating new theories, definitions and visions using rhetorical methods. In addition, these new definitions can draw attention to marginalized perspectives on rhetoric and new visions of women's and men's agency.

51

Empery: Winnet, Magma and Leia

Introduction

The purpose of this chapter is to present the collected empirical material from the three organizations Winnet, Magma and Leia. The description is structured based on the overarching scientific definition of social innovation used in this study, that is, the development of new goods, services, methods, ways of organizing and social structures that are social in their means and goals (cf. European Commission 2013a; Howaldt et al. 2015; Mulgan et al. 2007).

Winnet Sweden is a non-profit national umbrella organization with over 90 local and regional resource centres for women (RCs) around the country as member organizations. Already in the 1980s, RCs were established as part of the rural movement and the model was further developed in the 1990s with support from the Swedish Agency for Economic and Regional Development (then Nutek and the Swedish Agency for Sparsely Rural Areas) and subsequently spread to several other countries in Europe where there is now a European umbrella organization for resource centres: Winnet Europe. According to the Swedish Agency for Economic and Regional Development's program for RCs, their activities should contribute to gender-equal regional growth by making women's conditions visible and increasing women's influence in the following areas: 1) Entrepreneurship and innovative environments, 2) Skills supply and increased labor supply, 3) Accessibility, 4) Strategic cross-border cooperation, 5) Rural development. RCs offers, among other things, knowledge, training, advice, methods, meeting places and networks to two target groups: firstly, to individual women who want to realize their ideas for new companies, innovations, projects, etc., and secondly to politicians and civil servants who design and implement public initiatives for socially, ecologically and economically sustainable development in society. RC's activities are carried out through multi-level governance, involving many different actors from the public, private, idea-based and academic sectors, in *quadruple helix* constellations. (cf. Carayannis & Campbell 2010; Jonsson 2014; Lindberg et al. 2012, 2014).

Since 2002, RCs has had a mission from the Swedish Parliament and Government to highlight women's conditions and increase women's influence in regional growth efforts. The assignment states that the activities should promote knowledge transfer and knowledge development in close collaboration with county administrative boards, county councils and collaboration bodies, as well as with other relevant actors. Based on this assignment, the Swedish Agency for Economic and Regional Growth provides funds to RCs that are deemed to meet the assignment's criteria and guidelines, which, among other things, stipulate that they must use three working methods: 1) Critically examine and highlight the existing structures that limit women's influence and participation and worsen women's conditions within the framework of the five areas of focus, 2) Through collaboration, dialogue and dissemination activities, contribute to increased knowledge about the change work required to improve women's conditions and increase women's influence and participation in regional growth work, 3) Implement activities that contribute to increasing women's influence and participation and improve women's conditions within one or more areas of focus.

Magma is a non-profit organization that was founded in 2002 and that, through networks in various locations in Sweden (including Norrbotten, Västerbotten, Skåne and Stockholm) as well as Norway and Denmark, works for mutual support, inspiration and exchange of experiences between women active in culture, gender equality, diversity and entrepreneurship. Magma participants support each other socially and professionally by sharing their ideas, knowledge, contacts and life experiences. Together they create opportunities to realize dreams, projects and innovations through innovative collaborations, which has resulted in a number of new films, books, companies, job opportunities, etc. In Magma, women in their careers and women who are far from working life meet, which contributes new inspiration to already working women but also provides support to people who need a fresh start in their working life or private life due to sick leave, unemployment, disability or other reasons.

Leia corporate hotel is a limited liability company that was formed in 2013 as a result of a project run by the non-profit organization Magma Västerbotten with funding from, among others, the County Administrative Board of Västerbotten. When the *Leia Accelerator* project was initiated in 2010 with the aim of developing and testing a method for gender-equal companies (in the sense that they are at least half owned by women), another step was taken towards the establishment of the corporate hotel. The corporate hotel provides facilities and methods for entrepreneurs to develop through mutual inspiration. By sharing premises, entrepreneurs can have both spontaneous meetings in corridors and lunchrooms and planned meetings in offices and meeting rooms. This allows entrepreneurs to easily inspire and be inspired by each other. The shared premises aim to provide a professional setting for the companies, given that many of the entrepreneurs previously worked from home. The professional setting has been deliberately reinforced by designing and furnishing the premises based on Leia's graphic brand. In all of Leia's activities, a *coaching approach* is used, which means that each individual's own strengths, dreams and experiences are recognized and utilized. Leia has developed a special method to accelerate gender-equal entrepreneurship where success is built in teams and where entrepreneurs support each other's development processes through generous exchanges of experience.

Social innovation as a means and goals

Winnet

Winnet can be considered social in its goals in the sense that they should contribute to gender-equal regional growth by highlighting women's conditions and increasing women's influence in five areas: 1) Entrepreneurship and innovative environments, 2) Skills supply and increased labour supply, 3) Accessibility (IT, transportation, etc.), 4) Strategic cross-border cooperation (across geographical and organizational boundaries), 5) Rural development. Winnet Sweden's purpose statement states that the organization shall work to ensure that women take their share of society's resources, that women's skills are utilized in society, and that the contributions of women and men are valued equally. Parts of this are carried out within the framework of the Swedish Agency for Economic and Regional Growth's program *Resource Centers for Women.*[8] while other parts are carried out within the framework of other initiatives, such as the Swedish Agency for Economic and Regional Development's program *Promoting Women's Entrepreneurship.*[9] and the government's focus on women's organizing[10] .

Winnet is social in its means in the sense that it provides individual women as well as politicians and civil servants with knowledge, training, advice, methods, meeting places and networks. Since its inception, RCs have functioned as grassroots organizations that mobilize and organize women to increase their participation and influence in regional growth efforts. At the same time, the government's mission to RCs includes influencing and changing

---

[8]More info:
http://www.tillvaxtverket.se/huvudmeny/insatserfortillvaxt/regionalutveckling/jamstalld
regionaltillvaxt/resurscentraforkvinnor
[9]More info:
http://www.tillvaxtverket.se/huvudmeny/omtillvaxtverket/resultat/avslutadeprogram/fr
amjakvinnorsforetagande
[10]More info: http://www.mucf.se/bidrag-till-kvinnors-organisering

structures in the design and implementation of growth policy by influencing politicians and civil servants to change rules, programs, resource allocation, etc. In this way, a bottom-up and a top-down perspective are combined in RC's operations. Winnet Sweden also organizes collaborative networks with actors from the public, private, idea-based and academic sectors in so-called *quadruple helix* constellations (cf. Carayannis & Campbell 2010; Jonsson 2014; Lindberg et al. 2012, 2014). Unlike the *triple helix* model prescribed in government innovation policy, where the public, private and academic sectors collaborate, RCs also emphasize the importance of the idea-based sector for growth and innovation. This means that women's non-profit organizations, informal networks and social enterprises (which legally often constitute economic associations) become relevant in regional growth efforts.

Magma

Magma is social in its goals in the sense that they want to contribute to an equal society where women and men have the same space and influence in different spheres of society such as politics, business, media and culture. The ambition is that through Magma, women will be given a platform to take up influential positions in society, while participation in the network can also contribute to a fresh start in working life and private life, for example in the event of sick leave, unemployment or disability.

Magma is social in its means in the sense that they create a platform for women to support, inspire and exchange experiences with each other in the areas of culture, equality, diversity and entrepreneurship. The basic idea of Magma is generosity in the sense that everyone generously shares ideas, knowledge, contacts and life experiences. Through these exchanges members grow together.

Leia

Leia Företagshotell is social in its goals in the sense that they work for equal and fair entrepreneurship and innovation, as well as for an equal labor market for those who have difficulty entering the workforce.

An example of how Leia contributes to creating gender-equal entrepreneurship is the corporate hotel's permissive environment, which helps entrepreneurs strengthen their self-image and self-confidence as entrepreneurs. Among other things, entrepreneurs receive role models by meeting people who already run their own businesses, expanded networks with other entrepreneurs and other relevant actors, and the opportunity to participate in seminars for increased knowledge and inspiration.

An example of how Leia contributes to creating equal entrepreneurship is the project *Entrepreneurship for All* that was carried out at Leia and which was aimed at foreign-born women who wanted to start a business, where an important part was that the teaching was done in easy Swedish. Previously, the *Leia Näring* project was also run, of which *Leia Forum* was part. It was a café for foreign-born women who wanted to discuss a business idea or needed inspiration to start their own businesses. Finding motivation and being able to see oneself as an entrepreneur were important components and the participants were able to improve their self-confidence with the help of the group.

An example of how Leia contributes to creating an equal labour market is *Yoda* , which is an organization where people who are far from the labour market due to unemployment, sick leave or disability are given a chance to enter working life. All participants in Yoda undergo training in Leia's coaching approach so they can perform administrative tasks for the entrepreneurs who rent offices in Leia. Yoda thus creates a "win-win situation" where participants gain skills and experience in working life that they would not otherwise have had access to, and the companies at Leia gain access to practical support, for example in the form of administrative services that they would not otherwise be able to afford. This is how Yoda is described by Leia's representatives:

"We can really deliver parts of what the employment agency can't, such as contacts and references and getting out and making yourself known. ... generally we manage to get good internships, which lead to added value..." (Seminar 7 May 2014).

Leia is social in its means in the sense that their method of business development consists of mutual inspiration and collaboration between entrepreneurs. The social aspect also consists of their coaching approach that permeates all their activities, where participants gain insight into their own strengths, dreams and experiences.

An example of how Leia is social in its means is the *Leia Accelerator* project, where a method for accelerating gender-equal entrepreneurship was developed by and with entrepreneurial women. The project was motivated by the fact that there was a need among entrepreneurial women in Umeå and Västerbotten for a business-promoting environment created based on norms other than the masculine norms that the entrepreneurs experienced characterized existing business-supporting environments. The values conveyed at Leia are that business development does not have to be about risks, competition and elitism, but can instead be about opportunities, collaboration and inclusion. When entrepreneurs dare to be open with their thoughts, experiences and strategies, they can inspire and be inspired by each other to further develop their companies. The goal of the method is for entrepreneurs at Leia to feel more confident and self-evident in their identity as entrepreneurs. The method is based on four strategies:

flexibility, expanded networks, collaboration, and a process from a single-sex to a multi-sex environment. Four components are included in the method: meeting place, coaching, seminars, conceptualization.

Other examples of how Leia is social in its means are the activities *Yoda* , *Leia Forum* and *Entrepreneurship for All* described in the previous section, where disadvantaged or underrepresented groups are given the chance to develop in working life through employment or entrepreneurship. Within the framework of *Yoda*, opportunities for synergy effects are identified between these areas:

"An ability or knowledge in oneself that one has not discovered through traditional channels (e.g. the Swedish Public Employment Service) can, in the longer term, give rise to ideas that one can create a job. We broaden their horizons of opportunity. Many who apply to Leia and Yoda have a curiosity about entrepreneurship and are attracted by our environment. I know more people who have plans to start businesses..." (Seminar 7 May 2014).

Social innovation as new social structures

Winnet
Winnet develops new social structures in the sense that their operations aim to contribute to gender-equal regional growth by highlighting women's conditions and increasing women's influence. By combining a bottom-up and top-down perspective, they want to contribute to creating a social structure that enables women and men to realize their ideas on equal terms, both through direct support for marginalized groups and through political change. Winnet's multi-level governance has the ambition to influence politics at local, regional, national and international levels. They have used the legitimacy created through Winnet's successes at the European level to influence national and regional politics.

Magma

Magma develops new social structures in the sense that they strive for an equal society where women and men have the same space and influence in different spheres of society (politics, business, media and culture). Through its networks, Magma has created a structure for mutual support, inspiration and exchange of experiences between women active in culture, equality, diversity and entrepreneurship.

Magma was founded with the vision of changing gender structures in society, where they felt that women too often compete with each other instead of supporting each other. They thereby want to change the social structures that they believe disadvantage women. Magmas encourages women to empower each other and grow together to become a strong enough force together to achieve social change.

Leia

Leia develops new social structures in the sense that their operations have the ambition to contribute to gender-equal and equal entrepreneurship and working life. They want to broaden the definition of business development and growth from primarily being about increased turnover and an increased number of employees to also include other types of development, such as increased collaboration between companies, increased use of external services, etc. They ultimately want to contribute to entrepreneurship and financial independence being seen as just as obvious for women as for men. The coaching approach that Leia uses in all her businesses can also be seen as a new social structure through its emphasis on collaboration and mutual inspiration instead of competition between entrepreneurs.

Social innovation as new ways of organizing

Winnet

Winnet Sweden's member organizations develop new ways of organizing by initiating and further developing resource centers at local, regional, national and international levels. The resource center model was invented, as previously mentioned, in Sweden and then spread to other parts of Europe and the world.

Several of the collaborative networks that Winnet initiates through its activities can be considered innovative both in terms of organizational methods and content. For example, they have further developed *the triple helix* into *the quadruple helix* as an organizational form for innovation networks to take advantage of the role of small businesses and the idea-based sector. Winnet Norrbotten has created a political network that brings together municipal councilors, county councilors and civil servants to discuss and act on local and regional gender equality issues. Nationally, Winnet Sweden has initiated *the Winnet Centre of Excellence*, which systematically connects member organisations to researchers with specialist expertise within the five areas of activity specified in the Swedish Agency for Economic and Regional Development's R& programme. They have also initiated and participated in several international collaborative projects for gender equality in business, the labor market, technological development, etc. One example s the project *Winnet 8* within the EU's *Interreg IVC* program with eight European countries that Winnet Sweden initiated at the request of the EU Commission and whose results are now being disseminated within *the Baltic Sea Strategy* and its action plan. As a result, the Winnet Center of Excellence in the Baltic Sea has The region was established in 2014.

Magma

Magma develops new ways of organizing by functioning as an innovative meeting place both via digital and physical forums. Magma has a joint website, Facebook page, LinkedIn page, Instagram account and an electronic newsletter where Magma's own events, members' activities and other relevant news and activities are marketed. They also arrange physical meetings in the form of lunch seminars, study circles, lectures, etc.

Since its inception, Magma has constantly developed its networks and is now present in several locations in Sweden (including Kiruna, Luleå, Boden, Skellefteå, Umeå, Stockholm, Malmö), Denmark (Copenhagen) and Norway (Bodö). Previously, Magma was divided into regional associations (e.g. Magma Syd, Magma Västerbotten, Magma Norrbotten, etc.). Today, these associations have merged into a single national organization where the various nodes in the country instead interact via Facebook groups and other digital media.

Over time, new organizations have spun off from Magma, for example in Västerbotten where the then regional association initiated the *Leia Accelerator* project where a corporate hotel was created to accelerate gender-equal entrepreneurship. After the project, the operation was made permanent in a limited company – Leia Företagshotell AB – which is jointly owned by several of the entrepreneurs who have rented the corporate hotel. More information about this can be found in the section about Leia.

Leia

Leia has continuously developed new ways of organizing, including by having been initiated as a temporary project that was then transformed into a permanent limited company. Creating a limited liability company was the result of careful consideration of the pros and cons of different organizational forms. In line with

Leia's collaboration strategy, all entrepreneurs in the corporate hotel were offered the opportunity to become partners in the limited company, resulting in six of them now co-owning the company. *Yooa* is also in the process of being further developed from a temporary operation to a permanent organization and is now a separate profit centre within Leia, with influence and participation from the participants without them having to risk their compensation from unemployment insurance funds as would be the case if they became partners in a social enterprise.

Leia has also consciously inspired the entrepreneurs in the corporate hotel to create new joint concepts and companies. One of the components of Leia's method for accelerating gender-equal companies is so-called *conceptualization*, which involves developing common concepts between the entrepreneurs at Leia in the form of, for example, activities, brands, projects or new companies. One example is the constellation of health entrepreneurs at the corporate hotel who created the joint brand *Sustainable Health*. Within the framework of the brand, the entrepreneurs arranged joint marketing activities and had plans to offer joint services for sale.

Social innovation as new methods

Winnet
Winnet develops new methods at a structural, general and specific level. At the structural level, they develop methods to influence politicians and decision-makers to contribute to equitable regional growth. At the general level, they develop methods for mapping the distribution of resources between actors, industries and types of innovation in regional growth policy, methods for gender-conscious innovation and business promotion, methods for gender-conscious employment services, etc. At the specific level, they develop methods for increased gender equality in working life, business and society, such as *the Gender Equality Map, the Gender*

Hand, the Mentor Ring, Foqus Business, Gender Guidance, Success Teams, etc.

The Gender Hand is a method for gender-aware business advice developed in collaboration between local and regional RCs in Dalarna. It shows in a concrete way how business advisors can treat both women and men in a less gender stereotypical way and thus better help them realize their ideas, regardless of industry, background or type of business idea. RC has also developed methods for this in other parts of the country.

Winnet Gävleborg and Winnet Norrbotten have developed methods for gender-aware employment placement that aim to break the gender-segregated labor market and increase the opportunities for both women and men to become an active part of working life based on their own specific interests and skills. Winnet Gävleborg has trained employment agents in a gender perspective for equal guidance, and in a pilot case tested and implemented this in groups with young women and men. This builds on previous results from the *Partnership for Gender Equality project in Gävleborg,* which was funded under the EU's *Equal* program. Winnet Norrbotten trains all of the county's employment agents in gender-equal guidance to improve women's and men's opportunities to make less gender-stereotypical career choices.

Magma

Magma develops new methods in the form of different concepts for mutual inspiration and exchange of experiences between members.

Magma Mitt i Maten is a concept where Magma members get to give a talk during lunch to create contacts, exchange ideas and knowledge, including about women's situation to increase gender equality in working life, business and society.

Another concept is *PechaKucha Nights* , which Magma arranges together with Svensk Form and LTU Business. It is a presentation concept that was developed in Japan where the speaker is allowed to present a theme of their choice with 20 images of 20 seconds each in a concise, interesting and inspiring way.

Two more concepts are *the Magma Prize of the Year* and *the Magma Woman of the Year* . To highlight women's activities and skills, Magma presents *the Magma Prize of the Year* as an award to the person chosen as *Magma Woman of the Year* . The award is given to a woman who has done something unique for Norrbotten within one or more of Magma's areas of operation. The prize is designed by the members themselves, who are invited to submit entries to an exhibition where a jury selects see this year's winning artwork.

Leia

Leia develops new methods in the form of, for example, an innovative method for accelerating gender-equal entrepreneurship, which was described in previous sections. *Yoda* can also be considered an innovative method for meeting needs, both among the entrepreneurs at Leia and among people who are far from the labor market. Within *Leia Forum* and *Entrepreneurship for All*, methods for equal entrepreneurship have been developed, where foreign-born women receive inspiration and tools to start their own business. Leia has also developed a method for mixing and matching different companies and industries at the corporate hotel to inspire new innovative collaborations. The idea is that differences enrich and provide opportunities for business development and innovation.

The meeting place that Leia Företagshotell constitutes is also a central method for all of Leia's operations. The lunchroom serves as a meeting place for spontaneous meetings, exchange of experiences and mutual inspiration. Instead of the entrepreneurs sitting alone at home and working, there is the opportunity to go to a lunch room and meet others, which was one reason why standing tables were placed there. This is how this method is described by Leia representatives:

"Meeting place was exactly the word we had in mind when we drew what it would look like. The opposite of sitting at home and working alone was being able to go to a lunchroom. Stopping at a standing desk on the way to the photocopier... all meetings." (Seminar 7 May 2014).

Social innovation as new goods and services

Winnet
Winnet Sweden's member organizations develop new goods and services in a variety of forms, both themselves and through the ideas that they enable women to realize.

The Gender Equality Map is a service developed by Winnet Västra Götaland to identify unequal places and activities in a municipality or region, by visualizing them on a map:

"The problem with people discussing gender equality is that they mix (...) apples and oranges. Therefore, we need to find a common platform. Therefore, *the Gender Equality Map* is based on a selection of indicators that are objective in the sense that they are statistical. "(The map) is visualized with various equality parameters, such as services in municipalities, so that municipal residents and politicians can see what needs to be done." (Seminar 7 May 2014).

The gender equality map also includes two interactive maps: *The Safety Map* and *the Travel Habit Map*. Via *the Safety Map,* women and men can communicate to authorities how they experience different places in public space from a safety perspective. Via *the Travel Habit Map,* residents can provide information about their travel patterns, i.e. which routes they travel, which means of transport they use and the purpose of their trips. This can form the basis for decisions about how society should be designed with new roads, public transport, shopping centres, street lighting, etc.

Another service developed by KvinnoCenter in Bergsjön is *Cultural Interpreters*, which consist of foreign-born women who have lived in Sweden for a long time and help newly arrived women communicate with, for example, the school so that the children can meet the learning objectives. In this way, the knowledge of immigrant women is utilized, and a need is filled in a way that other social actors have not been able to do. It also serves as a step towards self-sufficiency for the cultural interpreters.

BalticFem has developed a mobile app for cycle tourists in the Baltic Sea archipelago environments (Sweden, Finland, Estonia) that connects IT and tourism, that is, a technical male-dominated area with a service-based gender-balanced area. In a *quadruple helix* collaboration between small businesses, researchers, non-profit organizations and authorities, new mobile solutions were developed that met the needs of IT companies, tourism companies and tourists.

Magma

Magma develops new goods and services through the realization of a series of ideas by the participants, both individually and collectively, through the inspiration that the participants have given each other through Magma's activities.

For example, Magma has published two anthologies with first-hand stories written by Magma members: *Cackling* and *More Cackling* . A third anthology is now being planned with the working title *End of Cakling? Absolutely not!* The members' diverse skills have been utilized in the production of the anthologies. They have been written, illustrated, edited and designed by members. They have also been published by publishing houses run by members (Ordsmedjans Förlag in Trunnerup, Skåne, and Lumio Förlag in Hedenäset outside Övertorneå, Norrbotten). After participating in Magma's anthologies, several members have gained inspiration and confidence to publish their own books and start their own publishing houses. An example is Anne-Christine Liinanki, who published the reportage book *Norrbotten lives, isolated* together with photographer Gunnar Svedenbäck. Together they now run the publishing house Aquilonis Book Publishing. She has also published the novel *Storsie* and taken a film script course and written a film script in collaboration with Filmpool Nord.

After meeting at Magma's activities, some of the participants have created joint films. An example is the film *I Am My Own Dolly Parton,* where documentary filmmaker Jessica Nettelbladt documented five musicians who planned a joint tribute concert to Dolly Parton and then shared their innermost dreams and fears about their work and private lives. Another documentary film created with Magma as its starting point is *Lönnsboda Fox*, where several members contributed in different ways: one filmed, one subtitled the film, and another handled the marketing.

Rosa and Asor are further examples of products developed with a starting point in Magma, where members have written and illustrated comic books and films about gender identity and exclusion based on a story about a pair of Siamese twins, aimed at a young audience.

Leia

Leia develops new products and services both in the corporate hotel as a whole and among the entrepreneurs who use the corporate hotel's premises. Since the entrepreneurs are primarily active in-service industries, it is mainly new services that have been developed. These have been developed both individually and jointly by various entrepreneurs in the corporate hotel.

Analysis: Empowerment within Social Innovation

Introduction
The analysis helps answer the study's three questions: 11) How is empowerment within social innovation expressed in the organizations studied? 2) How can participatory research approach help identify the opportunities and limitations of empowerment in innovation? 3) How can previous research on social innovation and empowerment contribute to identifying the opportunities and limitations of the empowerment within innovation perspective? The analysis encompasses empowerment within innovation at the individual level (micro level), organizational level (meso level) and societal level (macro level) to capture the complexity of the process of social inclusion that characterizes social innovation (cf. Cajaiba-Santana 2014; Dawson & Daniel 2010; Moulaert et al. 2005). This is achieved through rhetorical methods combined with previous research on social innovation, empowerment and innovation. The chapter concludes with a reflection on the possibilities and limitations of the perspective.

Empowerment within social innovation in the studied organizations
This section analyses the study's first question about how social innovation is expressed in the organizations studied. This is done using the rhetorical methods described in the methods chapter: rhetorical cluster method and rhetorical gender method. Using the rhetorical cluster method, statements and activities from the studied organizations are distinguished that are related to the process of social inclusion that, according to previous research, is central to social innovation (cf. Cajaiba-Santana 2014; Dawson & Daniel 2010; Moulaert et al. 2005). These statements and activities are then categorized using the rhetorical method to discern the movement towards inclusion using the categorizations *reformulation (O), restatement (Å), new visions (N).*

When organizations' innovation development is analyzed using rhetorical methods, the following patterns are discerned:

1) *Reformulation* includes the organizations' efforts to make visible and change differences in women's and men's access to meeting places (rooms), resources, influence, etc. Winnet, for example, works to ensure that women can claim their share of growth policy resources and strives to ensure that women's and men's efforts in entrepreneurship, innovation, etc. are valued equally. Magma has the ambition to contribute to an equal society where both women and men have the same space and influence in different spheres of society (politics, business, culture, etc.). Leia works for an equal business and labor market where people who are far from the labor market are supported to find their place in working life.

Examples from empirical research:
Winnet: Contribute to gender-equal regional growth by highlighting women's conditions and increasing women's influence *(O)*
Winnet: Make women's conditions visible and increase women's influence in regional growth efforts *(O and Å)*
Winnet: Three working modes: 1) Critically examine and highlight the existing structures that limit women's influence and participation and worsen women's conditions... *(O)*[11]
Winnet: Work to ensure that women take their share of society's resources... that women's skills are utilized in society... that women's and men's contributions are valued equally *(O)*

---

[11]"..." means that the meaningful part has been sorted out. This means that the sentences in their entirety can be found in the empirical chapter.

Winnet: Making women's conditions visible and increasing women's influence... Direct support to marginalized groups through political change *(O and Å)*

Magma: Share your ideas, knowledge, contacts and life experiences *(O and Å)*

Magma: Contribute to an equal society where women and men have the same space and influence in different spheres of society such as politics, business, media and culture *(O and Å)*

Magma: (... Change that) women too often compete with each other instead of supporting each other *(O)*

Magma: New social structures in the sense that they strive for an equal society where women and men have the same space and influence... (politics, business, media and culture) *(O and Å)*

Find: Develop and test a method for gender-equal companies in the sense that they are at least half owned by women *(O and Å)*

Find: The corporate hotel provides premises and methods for entrepreneurs to develop through mutual inspiration... Given that many of the entrepreneurs previously worked from home *(O and Å)*

Find: Works for equal and fair entrepreneurship and innovation, as well as for an equal labor market for those who have difficulty entering the workforce *(O and Å)*

2) *Re-engagement* includes making marginalized perspectives such as those of women and civil society visible in the field of innovation. Winnet presents its members' contributions and perspectives within the working world and the business community to politicians and civil servants who design and implement public growth initiatives. Magma's members jointly create innovations through innovative collaborations that have resulted in books, films, companies, job opportunities, etc. In Leia, entrepreneurs support each other's development processes through mutual inspiration and exchange of experiences, where new knowledge, collaborations and products are created.

Examples from empirical research:

Winnet: RCs offers, among other things, knowledge, training, advice, methods and meeting places and networks to two target groups: firstly to individual women... and secondly to politicians and civil servants who design and implement public initiatives for socially, ecologically and economically sustainable development in society *(Á)*

Winnet: Many actors are involved from the public, private, idea-based and academic sectors *(Å)*

Winnet: Make women's conditions visible and increase women's influence in regional growth efforts *(O and Å)*

Winnet: Promote knowledge transfer and knowledge development in close collaboration with county administrative boards, county councils and collaboration bodies *(Å)*

Winnet: 2) Through collaboration, dialogue and dissemination activities, contribute to increased knowledge about the change work required to improve women's conditions and increase women's influence and participation in regional growth work *(Å)*

Winnet: 3) Implement activities that contribute to increasing women's influence and participation *(Å)*

Winnet: Contribute to gender-equal regional growth... make women's conditions visible.... Entrepreneurship and innovative environments... strategic cross-border collaboration across geographical and organizational boundaries *(Å)*

Winnet: Mobilize and organize women to increase their participation and influence in regional growth efforts *(Å)*

Winnet: Making women's conditions visible and increasing women's influence... Direct support to marginalized groups through political change *(O and Å)*

Winnet: Collaboration projects for gender equality in business, the labor market, technological development, etc. *(Å)*

Winnet: Influence politicians and decision-makers to contribute to gender-equal regional growth *(Å)*

Winnet: Resource distribution between actors, industries and types of innovation in regional growth policy *(Å)*

Winnet: Gender-aware employment services that aim to break the gender-segregated labor market *(Å and N)*

Winnet: Common platform: The equality map... is visualized with different equality parameters... The safety map... communicates to authorities how they experience different places in public space *(Å)*

Magma: Works for mutual support, inspiration and exchange of experiences... *(Å)*

Magma: Share your ideas, knowledge, contacts and life experiences *(O and Å)*

Magma: Innovations through innovative collaborations (in new books, films, companies and jobs) *(Å)*

Magma: In Magma, women in their careers and women who are far from working life meet *(Å)*

Magma: Contribute to an equal society where women and men have the same space and influence in different spheres of society such as politics, business, media and culture *(O and Å)*

Magma: Women through magma will be given a platform to be able to take up influential positions in society *(Å)*

Magma: Generosity in the sense that everyone generously shares ideas, knowledge, contacts and life experiences *(Å)*

Magma: New social structures in the sense that they strive for an equal society where women and men have the same space and influence... (politics, business, media and culture) *(O, Å, N)*

Magma: Ideas have been realized by the participants, both individually and collectively through the inspiration that the participants have given each other through Magma's activities *(Å)*

Find: Develop and test a method for gender-equal companies in the sense that they are at least half owned by women *(O and Å)*

Find: The corporate hotel provides premises and methods for entrepreneurs to develop through mutual inspiration... Given that many of the entrepreneurs previously worked from home *(O and Å)*

Find: Coaching approach, which means that each individual's own strengths, dreams and experiences are recognized and utilized *(Å)*

Find: Entrepreneurs support each other's development processes through generous exchanges of experience *(Å)*

Find: Works for equal and fair entrepreneurship and innovation, as well as for an equal labor market for those who have difficulty entering the workforce *(O and Å)*

Find: The corporate hotel's permissive environment helps entrepreneurs strengthen their self-image and self-confidence as entrepreneurs... role models... participate in seminars for increased knowledge and inspiration *(Å)*

3) *New visions* include the creation of new theories, definitions and visions using innovative solutions. In Winnet, this involves, among other things, creating new innovation constellations such as *the quadruple helix* where civil society's contribution to innovation development is utilized in addition to that of business, government and academia. In Leia, a new kind of business promotion method and innovative environment has been developed based on the insight that entrepreneurship and innovation do not need to be based on the masculine normative focus on risks, competition and elitism, but can be about opportunities, collaboration and inclusion.

Examples from empirical research:

Magma: New social structures in the sense that they strive for an equal society where women and men have the same space and influence... (politics, business, media and culture) *(O, Å, N)*

Winnet: Bottom-up and top-down perspectives... *Quadruple helix* constellations... unlike the *triple-helix* model prescribed in state innovation policy, where public, private and academic sectors collaborate, RCs also emphasize the importance of the idea-based sector for growth and innovation *(N)*

Winnet: The gender hand – business advisors can treat both women and men in a less gender stereotypical way *(N)*

Winnet: Gender-aware employment services that aim to break the gender-segregated labor market *(Å and N)*

Leia Forum – a café for foreign-born women who wanted to discuss a business idea or needed inspiration to start their own businesses *(N)*

Find: Yoda, which is an activity where people who are far from the labor market due to unemployment, sick leave or disability are given a chance to enter working life *(N)*

Find: Leia Accelerator... business-promoting environment created based on non-masculine norms... The values conveyed at Leia are that business development does not have to be about risks, competition or elitism but can be about opportunities, collaboration and inclusion... Broaden the definition of business development... increased collaboration between companies, increased use of external services etc. *(N)*

Find: Leia has also developed a method for mixing and matching different companies and industries at the corporate hotel to inspire new innovative collaborations *(N and Å)*

When Winnet, Magma and Leia's social innovation processes are analyzed using the rhetorical methods above, the following relationship between reformulation, restatement and new visions emerges (see Table 1.1 below).

Table 1.1 Reformulation, restatement and new visions in organizations' development of empowerment within social innovation

Strategy/Org.	W	M	L	
O	10 (16%)	4 (6%)	3 (5%)	17 (27%)
Å	22 (35%)	9 (14%)	7 (11%)	38 (60%)
N	3 (5%)	1 (2%)	4 (6%)	8 (13%)
Tot.	35 (56%)	14 (22%)	14 (22%)	63 (100%)

O = Reformulation, Å = Retraction, N= New visions.
W = Winnet, M = Magma, L= Leia.

Winnet primarily uses re-engagement as a rhetorical strategy in its activities (35%), which is about creating platforms and resources to make visible women's existing and potential contributions to working life, entrepreneurship and innovation. Among these strategies is the strategy to promote knowledge transfer and knowledge development about women's conditions in working life and business, in close collaboration with authorities and collaboration bodies. Winnet also uses a reformulating strategy (16%) where, among other things, through the Equality and Safety Maps they show the differences between women's and men's access to transport, safety in different places, etc. In some cases, Winnet uses New Visions (5%): as a theoretical and practical extension of the innovation concept - *quadruple helix* constellation. Magma primarily uses a reciprocating strategy (14%) which includes generously sharing ideas, knowledge, contacts and life experiences with other women, to increase inclusion in working life, business and social life. Magma uses reframing (6%) by getting women to collaborate instead of competing. Magma uses the New Visions strategy to some extent (2%). Leia is the organization that uses new visions as a strategy to the greatest extent (6%), by creating new language, mindsets and working methods through activities such as Leia Accelerator, Leia Forum and Yoda, etc. Leia uses reframing (and reframing) when the organization provides meeting places and rooms where many of the entrepreneurs previously worked from home - a way to show women's and men's working patterns (5%). Leia uses reintegration when supporting each other's development processes - resource utilization - through continuous exchange of experiences (11%),

Empowerment within Social Innovation at micro, meso and macro levels

To deepen the analysis of what empowerment within innovation means in the studied organizations, the above results are supplemented with an analysis based on previous research on micro-, meso- and macro-levels in social innovation (cf. Cajaiba-Santana 2014; Howaldt et al. 2015). Together, these perspectives make it possible to outline the movement from social exclusion to social inclusion that, according to previous research, is central to social innovation (cf. Cajaiba-Santana 2014; Dawson & Daniel 2010; Moulaert et al. 2005).

The above analysis shows that the organizations work to different extents in different contexts and at different levels (cf. Howaldt et al. 2015). Winnet is the organization that operates in the most different forums from local to EU level with the oldest history and spread, which certainly contributes to them representing all three strategies (*reformulation, re-entry* and *new visions*). In that sense, Leia is the latest addition as they are a spin-off from Magma and work primarily with new visions. In its strategies and organizational choices, Magma has adopted a gender strategy where they focus on strengthening individuals' opportunities for and in their careers. Winnet's ambition at *the macro level* is to contribute to gender-equal regional growth by highlighting women's conditions and increasing women's influence. By combining a bottom-up and a top-down perspective, they want to create a new social structure that will enable women and men to realize their ideas on equal terms, both through direct support for marginalized groups of women and through influencing politicians and civil servants. Magma's ambition at *the macro level* is to contribute to an equal society where women and men have the same space and influence in various spheres of society, such as politics, business, media and culture. The digital and physical meeting places that Magma creates are intended to help women support, inspire and exchange experiences with each other instead of competing. Leia's ambition at *a macro level* is to contribute to a gender-equal and equal business and working life, which is reflected in the project *Entrepreneurship for All*, where foreign-born women are supported to start businesses, and in *Yoaa*, where entrepreneurs gain access to administrative services while the unemployed/sick people have a chance to enter the labour market.

The organizations studied have created structures to influence decision-makers. They use strategies to highlight how new arenas can be created, differences in society's resource distribution between women and men, and how to visionary change society (i.e., *reformulation, re-enactment, and new visions*).

The organizations studied work against and with complex structures through norm change at *the societal level*. Winnet's activities aim to create gender-equal regional growth by highlighting and utilizing women's skills and experiences to change politics in a more gender-equal direction. Which is about *retaking* and *reformulating* strategies. *The macro level* is influenced by initiatives at *the meso level*. Among other things, Winnet participates in the formulation and review of regional and national strategies and action plans for growth, innovation, working life development, rural development, etc.

Magma's basic strategy of paying it forward means that when members have been helped or inspired by someone, they use their gratitude to help or inspire someone else, instead of just saying thank you to the person they have been helped or inspired by. This way, the benefits are spread to significantly more people than just those who initially gave and received the help. At the micro level, organizational strategies express that by sharing their life experiences of both sadness and joy, the effect is that even more people want to share with even more people. This is an example of how the three levels are woven together by the act of passing on at *the micro level* being facilitated by Magma's activities at *the meso level*, which in turn can change the conditions for women's scope for action at *the macro level*. Leia's coaching approach recognizes and utilizes everyone's own strengths, dreams and experiences, and the method for accelerating equal entrepreneurship is based on opportunities, collaboration and inclusion instead of risks, competition and elitism (*reframing* and *retaking*). Leia's coaching at the micro level builds an understanding of how other companies at *the meso level* can work.

The organizations also have the ambition to contribute to local and regional development at *a macro level*, as Winnet's efforts have also been utilized at a European level, where their operating model and message have been adopted by several different actors, which has resulted in resource centers for women being established in several countries based on the model developed in Sweden. Another example is Magma's effort for women to strengthen each other and grow together to become a strong enough force to bring about *social change* . According to Magma, when women and men are given the same space and influence in different spheres of society, such as politics, business, media and culture, regions become attractive as living environments for both women and men. Leia's ambition is that entrepreneurship and financial independence should be seen as just as obvious for women as for men. Since the start, they have had the goal of putting Umeå and Västerbotten on the map as a region for gender-equal entrepreneurship. As part of this, they have strived to become an obvious reference body for municipal and regional authorities on issues of entrepreneurship, innovation, diversity and equality. The analysis above is about *reformulation*.

By working on innovative thinking around the inclusion of perspectives and actors, *the meso level* can be a springboard for changes at *the macro level*, which can be seen as a development of work processes. This can be exemplified by Winnet's further development of *the triple helix* into *the quadruple helix* (cf. Lindberg et al. 2012, Lindberg 2015b). This is an organizational form for innovation networks to utilize the contribution of small businesses and the idea-driven sector to innovation development (cf. Lindberg et al. 2014). *The Winnet Centre of Excellence* is also an example of reorganising work processes where researchers and RCs meet to exchange knowledge and experience to influence policy and its implementation in a gender-equal direction. Magma's efforts to ensure that women support, inspire and exchange experiences with each other in both private and working life are shaped within the framework of the meeting places that Magma organizes. By giving women who would otherwise probably not have met the opportunity to do so, unexpected inspiration can arise across social and geographical boundaries. For example, a woman in the middle of her career can inspire and be inspired by a woman who is long-term unemployed but perhaps at the same time artistically creative. Strategically, the analysis above is about *new visions*.

Changes at *the meso level* can affect both *the micro* and *macro levels*, for example in Leia's case where development from a temporary project to a permanent limited company (and the prospect that *Yoda* will also undergo the same transformation) contributes to *the empowerment* of individuals but also structural changes. Furthermore, *Yoda* itself constitutes a way to reorganize work processes through its innovative combination of meeting entrepreneurs' needs for administrative services and the unemployed/sick/disabled's needs for work opportunities. This creates value for four parties: Leia gains added value for its tenants, companies receive training before hiring their own staff, the Swedish Public Employment Service and society gain more long-term unemployed and long-term sick leave holders who can return to work, and individuals gain increased opportunities in the labour market. Strategically, the four values create awareness – *reformulating* – society about the shortcomings of the labor market and about *reintegration* – bringing in other perspectives on the needs of the marginalized. This is seen in the possibilities for change in, for example, social policy. based on Winnet's operations. The activities consist primarily of enabling women who are far from the labour market due to sick leave, unemployment or disability to realize their ideas for entrepreneurship, work or other things through counselling, education, networking, etc. Magma's way of changing the forms of social work and social policy consists primarily of their innovative way of giving members a fresh start in working life or private life in the event of, for example, sick leave, unemployment or disability. This is achieved through Magma's inclusive network where women in their careers can meet women who are far from the labour market and thus have the opportunity to help each other move forward in life. Leias consists primarily of the activities within *Yoda*, which in an innovative way enables people who are far from the labor market to have an adapted entrance to work. With Leia's coaching approach and inspiring environment, they get the chance to gain experience and contacts for future potential employment in property management, cleaning, offices, reception, etc. Changes for individuals in terms of their relationship to working life are a *micro-level change*, which is generated by *the meso-level* through organizations working with these changes, which can have an impact on how society works towards those who are far from the labour market at *the macro level*.

The organizations show that social innovations are a way to create social inclusion in the sense that individuals, organizations and communities are supported in the development of new practices that increase quality of life, well-being, relationships and empowerment. However, this does not mean that the organizations' activities are inclusive in every sense. The organizations mainly involve women, although men are involved to some extent as entrepreneurs in Leia and as target groups in authorities in Winnet and Magma. The focus on women is based on the marginalization of women as a group in the field of innovation (cf. Alsos and others 2013; Andersson et al. 2012; Lindberg & Schiffbänker 2013; Pettersson 2007), which the organizations strive to change from social exclusion to social inclusion. The organizations studied thus have an overall inclusive goal with their operations, but where exclusion is included to some extent. Even within the group of women, exclusion can be discerned in the organizations' activities, where it is mostly Swedish-born middle-class women who are involved. At the same time, all organizations have initiatives to expand the spectrum of participating women, where, for example, Leia's initiatives *Entrepreneurship for All* are aimed at foreign-born women based on their need for employment and contacts, and *Yoda* involves women (and men) who are far from the labour market due to long-term unemployment, long-term sick leave, etc. Similarly, Magma has the ambition to involve both women in their careers and women outside the labour market, in order to achieve mutually beneficial collaborations. Even in Winnet, foreign-born women are involved in certain local resource centres. These strategies described above are about *reintegration*, as the focus has been on making visible primarily women's perspectives. Although the organizations work to some extent with men as entrepreneurs.

Ultimately, organizations work primarily with *reformulation* at the macro level, with *new visions* at the meso level, and with *reintegration* at the micro level. The organizations work largely towards the macro level with the strategies. Their efforts - that they have - and give others - a skill to change the macro level as Gendered social innovation strategies are an attempt to influence the societal level from different directions and levels, as an *out-group innovation* where social groups try to change their situation by advocating structural change at the macro level (cf. Cajaiba-Santana 2014). However, there is a variation in strategies and levels, which may depend on which counterparts the work is directed towards, and which strategy is best suited at a certain level.

Participatory research approach for Empowerment within Social Innovation

This section answers the study's second question about how a participatory research approach can help identify the possibilities and limitations of the perspective.

The study process has shown how a participatory research approach can lower the thresholds for marginalized groups to participate in scientific knowledge development about innovation, in a way that can contribute to making society more inclusive in terms of the development of future solutions. By striving for an equal dialogue, the participatory research approach has contributed to increasing *empowerment* among the participating organizations, in the sense that they have thereby been able to increase their understanding of and scope for action to make innovation development visible and promote it in an inclusive manner (cf. Andersson 2012; Svensson et al. 2002). The organizations, in turn, have sought to empower marginalized groups to develop their social, economic and political capacity to realize their ideas (cf. Kabeer 2003; Nussbaum 2011; Sen 1999).

The project's seminars have functioned as a kind of knowledge-generating laboratory where Gendered social innovation has been explored and created as a kind of *boundary object* or *quasi-concept* (cf. Lindberg & Portinson Hylander 2017; Star 1988), which has contributed to understanding and managing the multifaceted and complex challenges and needs that the organizations have identified. This has created a local contextualization of the perspective that is both theoretically in-depth of innovation research and practically useful in the specific contexts of organizations. The bridging potential of social innovation as *a boundary object/quasi-concept* means that similar processes could be studied and pursued in other contexts based on the experiences presented in this study. As pointed out in the method chapter, *transferability* (cf. Herr & Andersson 2014) - created, with local adaptability, which is a form of both theoretical and practical dissemination. The organizations themselves continuously conduct dissemination processes around their activities in a few different forms, which can be distinguished in the analysis of the organizations' goods and services below.

The study process shows how empowerment within innovation can be documented and analysed using a participatory research approach where organizations' innovations have been framed in dialogue between researchers and participants. When different forms of knowledge (theoretical, practical and tacit knowledge) meet at the intersection of dialogue and participants' experiences, the correspondence with participants' experiences can be increased (cf. Bohlin 2009; Lindberg 2010; Wingblad & Jonsson 2009).

The participatory research approach has enabled documentation and analysis of organizations' efforts to increase *empowerment* for women in the field of innovation, even outside the boundaries of their own organization (cf. Kabeer 2003; Nussbaum 2011; Since 1999). This has been an attempt to create socially robust knowledge, where conclusions are reconciled with actors in the practical context in a way that considers marginalized groups and perspectives (cf. Gunnarsson 2007; Gunnarsson & Westberg 2006, 2008). The participatory research approach has noted that Winnet's efforts have been utilized within the EU, where they have had the opportunity to spread their operating model so that more resource centres have been formed internationally based on the Swedish model. Similarly, the participatory research approach has highlighted the need for women and men to have the same space and influence in different spheres of society, such as politics, business, media and culture, so that regions become more attractive as living environments for both women and men. Within Leia, the participatory research approach has drawn attention to the spread and effects of their activities regionally and nationally. Entrepreneurs in the inland have been offered to rent offices and premises at Leia as a showcase in the coastal region and that *Yoda* has recruited participants from the entire county, which could result in increased inclusion in the labour market and in the business community.

The participatory research approach has also enabled documentation and analysis of how organizations have developed innovative ways of organizing. This was achieved through, among other things, the participants' own studies of their own organizations through so-called *self-studies*, where the already established trust between researchers and organizations made it possible to produce the material (cf. Herr & Andersson 2014). These studies have, among other things, highlighted Winnet's development of *the quadruple helix* as an organizational form for innovation networks to be able to take advantage of the innovative power of small businesses and the idea-based sector. *The Winnet Centre of Excellence* is also an example of reorganising work processes where researchers and resource centres meet to exchange knowledge and experience to influence public investments in innovation, growth and regional development. From Magma's efforts for women's mutual support, inspiration and exchange of experiences in both private and working life, unexpected synergy effects have arisen with new collaborations across social and geographical boundaries. Leia's activities within *Yoda* constitute a new way of organizing through its innovative combination of meeting entrepreneurs' needs for administrative services and the unemployed/sick/disabled's needs for work opportunities.

The participatory research approach has also enabled documentation and analysis of how organizations develop and disseminate their innovations digitally. This has been made possible by reflecting on and analysing, for example, the organizations' methods and products to create practical and theoretically interesting knowledge - a form of craftsmanship in the spirit of Heidegger (cf. Furberg 2005; Wingblad & Jonsson 2008). Among other things, the organizations use various IT solutions for this, where, for example, Winnet's efforts to increase women's participation and influence in the IT area have been distinguished. Among other things, they have conducted several IT-focused projects at local, regional, national and international levels that have resulted in new apps, digital maps and marketplaces, and contributed a knowledge base to the government's digital agenda. Magma has created platforms for members to interact with each other and the outside world via Facebook, LinkedIn, etc. Leia has used digital technology in the form of Google Docs, Facebook, etc. to develop new business ideas and mutual inspiration for entrepreneurial development.

Finally, the participatory research approach has enabled documentation and analysis of how the organizations have strived to practically influence social structures in an equal direction, that is, to research "with" a knowledge-developing process (cf. (Aagaard Nielsin & Svensson 2006; Johannisson et al. 2008). This involved a kind of *conscientization* process (cf. Berglund & Danilda 2008) to strengthen the work of organizations and theorizing and developing the empowerment perspective. This partly consists of innovative solutions that could be spread to more social actors, which include Winnet's efforts as a catalyst for gender equality in regional growth work and methods for gender-aware employment and business advice, Magma's visibility of important women through *the Magma Woman of the Year* and Leia's coaching approach where each individual's own strengths, dreams and experiences are recognized and utilized. This partly consists of the organizations' efforts to influence politicians and authorities to contribute to gender equality in working life, business and society. This includes, among other things, Winnet's structure for political influence at local, regional, national and international levels to increase gender awareness in regional growth policy, Magma's efforts to highlight the importance of women in working life, business and regional development through networking, collaborations and role models, and Leia's efforts to create more inclusive structures in entrepreneurship and the labor market by inspiring cooperation instead of competition.

Theoretical contributions to Empowerment within Social Innovation

This section answers the third question about how previous research on social innovation, empowerment and innovation can help identify the opportunities and limitations of the perspective. In the spirit of Phelps (2007, 2013), the organizations have created creative environments where everyday knowledge and specialist knowledge can meet in different constellations, which was also reflected in the process where participatory methods were used to enable synergy effects between different forms of knowledge. Making visible other experiences and areas of activity than just technical innovation development in industrial companies demonstrates the innovative strategies of the organizations studied. To achieve this, the organizations studied have used a bottom-up approach (cf. Lindberg et al. 2012, 2014; Moulaert et al. 2005) where people are involved at the grassroots level, for example by using IT solutions like Magma to maintain contact between geographically separate parts of the organization in combination with physical meetings and lunch meetings where members can meet physically. These platforms and meetings are a great asset in gender equality work, as women have not had access to professional networks and the formal economy to the same extent as men (cf. Abrahamson 2000; Du Rietz 2013; Magnusson et al. 2008). In homes and in part-time jobs, not as many professional networks are cultivated as in working life, and therefore the organizations studied create platforms for women, but also to some extent for men, to be able to share each other's knowledge in solidarity, to support each other and give each other opportunities for resources and influence.

To discern how previous research can contribute to identifying the opportunities and limitations of the empowerment perspective, the movement from social exclusion to social inclusion is analyzed here based on three central aspects of social innovation identified in previous research on social innovation – 1) needs/challenges, 2) solutions and 3) improvements (cf. Cajaiba-Santana 2014; Dawson & Daniel 2010; Moulaert et al. 2005) – in relation to previous research. To further deepen the understanding of how previous research can contribute to understanding opportunities and limitations in empowerment-driven social innovation, the innovative aspects that, according to previous research, are central to the concept are also analysed: 4) the newness of an innovation 5) the specifically social newness 6) the normative newness and 7) the Gendered social newness (cf. Johnson Ross & Goddard 2015; Lindberg et al. 2015, 2016; Lindberg & Berglund 2016; Nahnfeldt & Lindberg, 2017).

Regarding the first aspect – identification of challenges and needs – the organizations have identified several gender-related *societal challenges and needs* of underrepresented and disadvantaged groups to increase gender equality in working life, business and regional development (cf. McGowan & Westley 2015; Moulaert et al. 2005), The organizations' solutions aim to *improve* for individuals, organizations and society by increasing gender equality in working life, business and regional development (cf. Cajaiba-Santana 2014; Howaldt et al. 2015), The organizations have developed a variety of innovative *solutions* in the form of new goods, services, methods, organizational forms and social structures to address identified needs and challenges (cf. Lindberg et al. 2015; Mulgan et al. 2007). Winnet draws attention to the fact that both women as a group and society at large have a need to make greater use of women's skills and experiences in public efforts for growth and innovation in order to achieve equal influence and benefit for women and men in regional development policy. Magma has identified the societal challenge of valuing the contributions of women and men equally and giving them the same space in different spheres of society (politics, business, media and culture). Leia sees a need for gender equality and equity in entrepreneurship, innovation and the labor market. These strategies correspond to the rhetorical strategies *of reformulation (R)* and *restatement (Å)*.

Regarding the second aspect – innovative solutions – Winnet has developed surveys, training, certifications and meeting places for cross-sector and cross-organizational mobilization, organizing, knowledge dissemination, job opportunities, influence, etc. Magma has developed physical and digital meeting places in the form of morning mingles, lunch lectures, exhibitions, awards, cultural productions, Facebook pages, etc. for mutual support and inspiration through the exchange of ideas, knowledge, experiences and contacts between women in different positions in working life and private life. Leia has established a corporate hotel, developed a social activity within the corporate hotel and an association for social entrepreneurship, as well as a coaching approach, a collaboration strategy where companies develop together, a mix strategy where different industries enrich each other and efforts to increase the inclusion of immigrant women in the labor market and business, etc. These strategies correspond to the rhetorical strategy *new visions (N)*.

The meeting places that have been created and organized in turn create language and tools for self-reflection and increased *empowerment* in a way that can help to distinguish and change prevailing gender patterns within innovation research (cf. Andersson 2012; Berglund & Danilda 2008; Svensson et al. 2002). These meeting places constitute a counterbalance to the male-dominated innovation networks that previously constituted the empirical focus of innovation research (cf. Alsos and others 2013; Andersson et al. 2012; Lindberg 2012; Lindberg & Schiffbänker 2013; Pettersson 2007). The organizations thus weave together professional and personal development in an innovative way, which highlights that the social dimensions of innovation must be studied in a multifaceted way (cf. Cajaiba-Santana 2014; Dawson & Daniel 2010; Moulaert et al. 2005). Examples of this are Leia's coaching approach with help-to-self-help for people who are far from the labor market and the design of the company hotel's lunchroom as a social arena where the private and professional meet to allow cross-border ideas to arise. Another example is the meetings that Magma creates between women in their careers and women who are unemployed, on sick leave or disabled, and Winnet's efforts for gender-equal regional development where structural and individual solutions to social needs and challenges are intertwined. The meeting places that organizations have created, where individuals' knowledge and experiences are focused, are a way to increase self-esteem and empowerment (cf. Kabeer 2003; Nussbaum 2011; Sen 1999). By treating knowledge and competence as something relational, that is, something that is created in dialogue between different people, the focus is on cooperation and mutual respect instead of expert knowledge and elitism. This relational approach is inclusive also by valuing the everyday knowledge and experiences of participants, as a counterbalance to the dominant valuation of technical and formal knowledge as most important for innovation development. This can help to shift the focus of innovation research away from elitism, competition and formal competence and thereby change the prevailing masculine norms in innovation research (cf. Alsos and others 2013; Andersson et al. 2012; Lindberg 2012; Pettersson 2007) in accordance with the theoretical perspective *of undoing gender* (cf. Deutsch 2007; Lindberg & Schiffbänker 2013) – a form of *new visions*.

Regarding the third aspect – social improvement – Winnet, for example, strives for gender-equal change in regional development, the labour market and entrepreneurship. Magma strives for changed gender structures in society, gender-equal regional development and attractive regions. Leia strives for equal and equitable entrepreneurship and working life combined with a new view of and new definitions of growth and entrepreneurial development. These strategies correspond to *retake (Å)* and *new visions (N)* . For example, social improvement can be seen in the platforms and network-based organizing methods that organizations have developed to mobilize and address the needs of underrepresented and disadvantaged groups. *Quadruple helix* (Carayannis & Campbell 2010; Jonsson 2014; Lindberg et al. 2012, 2014) is such an organizational method for collaboration between the private, public, academic and idea-driven sectors, which highlights the importance of both small businesswomen and women's organizations for innovation development. This reflects the theoretical perspectives of doing gender and *undoing gender* (cf. Abrahamsson 2000; Acker 1999; Deutsch 2007; Lindberg & Schiffbänker 2013; West & Zimmermann 1987) because it contributes to changing the understanding of how innovations develop, beyond segregating and hierarchical gender patterns. However, further knowledge and method development would be needed to deepen the understanding of how power relations and dissemination premises affect the scope for action of different groups and organizations to realize ideas for future solutions to social challenges and needs.

Regarding the fourth aspect - the novelty of an innovation - according to previous research (Cajaiba-Santana 2014; Howaldt et al. 2015; Lindberg & Berg Jansson 2016) consist of something that is new to the world, new to the context or new as a combination. In the empirical data analysed in this study, the new partly consists of things that can be considered completely new to the world (e.g. mobile app for cycle tourists, *Genushanden, Leia Forum/Leia Näring*), new to the context (e.g. *Magma Talks, Sustainable Health*) and new as a combination (e.g. Gender equality training for business advisors/employment agents , *Årets Magmapris/Magma Woman of the Year, Yoda*). The mobile app can be considered new to the world in the sense that it fulfils a common need among IT companies, tourism companies, and tourists that has not been previously met. *Sustainable Health* can be considered new to the context because a common brand was created for a constellation of health entrepreneurs, which was considered unusual in that industry. *This year's Magma Prize/Magma Woman* can be considered a new combination because previously known forms of highlighting and strengthening women's competence and exposure were combined in new concepts. The services and goods in the form of films, books, etc. that the organizations have created are not always innovative in themselves, but have often been created through innovative processes with new collaborative constellations, organizational forms, marketing channels, etc. The content of some of the goods and services can also contribute to social improvement by increasing gender awareness and equality in organizations and society, for example the books *Cackling* and *More Cakling,* which make women's experiences of the labor market, business and society visible, and *the Equality Map*, which makes gender patterns in different areas of society visible - *reintegration* and *new visions*.

The next aspect – the *specific social novelty* in the organizations' activities – can, according to previous research on social innovation, be distinguished in the form of new ways of identifying social needs and societal challenges, new ways of involving marginalized groups and perspectives in the development of innovation and new ways of creating social improvement for individuals, organizations and society new ways of collaborating between groups, organizations and sectors to identify and solve needs, which is also central to the social novelty (cf. Cajaiba-Santana 2014; Moualert et al. 2015; Mulgan et al. 2007; Petersson & Lindberg 2013; Lindberg & Berg Jansson 2016). In the organizations studied in this study, the socially new can be discerned, among other things, in the identification of the social needs of women as a group and the societal challenge to make greater use of women's knowledge and skills in public efforts for growth and innovation. It also consists of the development of new meeting places for the exchange of ideas, knowledge, experiences and contacts within and between different groups of women, decision-makers and innovation promoters. It also consists of creating social improvement for individuals, organizations and society through increased equality in working life, business and regional development. The social new can be seen in changes in the relationship between, for example, competition versus cooperation between people: instead of considering other entrepreneurs as competitors, Leia wants to encourage collaborative analyses of how different entrepreneurs can create synergies through collaboration. Magma's basic principle is mutual support and inspiration, both privately and professionally. Winnet's operations are built from a grassroots perspective where women help each other realize their goals and ideas. Innovation research's increasing focus on the importance of network structures for innovation development, including through *the triple helix* model, could, with inspiration from organizations, be expanded to include mutual support within marginalized groups, as a way of accumulating sufficient joint power to realize ideas and change existing organizational and societal structures (*new visions – N*).

The sixth aspect - the *normative novelty* of the organizatiors' activities - can, according to previous research on social innovation, be distinguished by analyzing from a power perspective the values that make a group disadvantaged or underrepresented in the field of innovation or by demonstrating the values that are required to increase the *empowerment* of this group (cf. Mulgan et al. 2007; Moualert et al. 2015; Lindberg et al. 2015). In the organizatiors studied, the issues include the norms that have contributed to marginalizing women's innovations and the organizations' innovative solutions to make women's innovations visible in research, politics and practice, as well as their alternatives to the prevailing masculire norms that can contribute to innovations in different sectors, industries and forms receiving the same status and priority (*O and Å*).

The normatively new can be seen in the grassroots perspective (bottom-up) that organizations use in their operations, and it can also inspire increased inclusion in innovation research (cf. Lindberg 2014, 2015a, 2015b; Lindberg et al. 2012, 2014; Moulaert et al. 2005). Winnet's mobilization of women at the local level to jointly formulate more equal paths to regional growth in dialogue with decision-makers, Magma's interweaving of the personal and professional to include marginalized women in, among other thincs, entrepreneurship and culture, and Leia's involvement of foreign-born women in her entrepreneurial development efforts constitute empirical examples of how innovation development can take place based on people's specific local needs with potential synergistic effects in cases where these local needs are linked to an organizational and/or societal level (*O and Å*).

It is precisely everyday knowledge that forms the very foundation of organizations' inclusive innovation perspectives. The organizations start from their members' identification of everyday needs and then develop the solutions that best fit the current context. Thereby, they circumvent dominant structures and ways of thinking in a way that contributes to increasing women's *empowerment* (cf. Kabeer 2003; Nussbaum 2011; Sen 1999). The activities that the organizations conduct thereby complement – and sometimes even replace – old institutions. Winnet has come the furthest in this process as they have managed to establish themselves as a knowledge resource for regional growth both locally, regionally, nationally and internationally. This process of change reflects the theoretical perspective of doing gender (cf. Abrahamsson 2000; Acker 1999; West & Zimmermann 1987) by making visible the differences in status and resources between women and men in the field of innovation and acting to equalize these differences. Such connections between individual everyday perspectives and structural societal perspectives could be studied within more inclusive forms of innovation research (N).

The last aspect - the Gendered social novelty in the organizations' activities - can be distinguished, based on previous research on gender aspects in social innovation, in the innovative identification and change of segregating and hierarchical gender patterns in organizations and society (cf. Lindberg & Berglund 2016; Lindberg et al. 2015, 2016). In Winnet, Magma and Leia, can primarily be distinguished in their sought-after reduction of gender-related segregation and hierarchy between different actors, sectors, industries and forms in the field of innovation. If the organizations' ambitions are realized, people, regardless of gender or field, would receive the same support in realizing their ideas for new goods, services, methods, organizational methods and social structures ($Å$ and O).

Final discussion on the perspective of Empowerment within Social Innovation

This study is written within a disciplinary tradition, with its epistemology and ontology: 1) A critical tradition and participatory method 2) Joint research initiation, *empowerment* and emancipation and 3) Theoretical and practical knowledge development through abduction. With these orientations, generalizability or the will to explain and predict are not the core of the scientific contribution, even if understanding and *transferability* are sub-goals of the study's democratic, dialogic, processual and cataclytical validity (cf. Herr & Andersson 2014). As shown in the method and analysis chapters, this study has an abductive approach where induction and deduction have been combined to create an understanding of the activities and actions of the studied organizations in relation to the newfound insights that the perspective provides. The concept has strengths from *the intention* to account for general attributes or characteristics in a concept, since the concept provides a theoretical tool for how an activity can be analysed based on needs/challenges, innovative solutions and improvements that are gender-equality *driven*, in the sense that they improve the basis for and the relationship between people. The concept also provides normative insight into what can produce a "good" society, which can be summarized with insights from inclusive innovation - where more perspectives, groups and individuals are given space for self-realization and societal benefit. The concept also has *extensive* strengths, to show the worldly phenomena that a concept constitutes, since the "parameters"/definition for the study were operationalized from social innovation theory, which is also the skeleton of the empirical chapter and guided the empirical collection. Thus, activities and phenomena that *do not* "belong" to the perspective *have not* been aggregated into facts (cf. Van Oosterhout & Heugens 2008). The results of the study can be used in other contexts if the conditions, actors and their actions of that context are considered. In other words, the epistemological focus of this study is that it considers context and theory simultaneously, to context because there is an interest in political, social, economic and cultural nuances and to theory because the possibilities and limitations of the concept have been analysed and because a form of local theory formation has been generated.

Conclusions and Prospects

Conclusions

Collaboration between researchers and stakeholders in scientific knowledge development based on an innovation science foundation has proven in this study to be a fruitful path to increased understanding of the theoretical and empirical conditions for studying the possibilities and limitations of using empowerment within innovation as a perspective on inclusive innovation. As a researcher, contributing to the development of a more complex understanding of social innovation in the practical experiences of the organizations concerned, as well as social science theories, is a unique opportunity thanks to the choice of participatory methods in the study process. The study's participatory knowledge development together with the three organizations Winnet, Magma and Leia contributes to further developing existing innovation research by showing how the perspective can be used to identify and analyse innovation development in a range of different forms, in many different arenas, by a diversity of actors. This enables more inclusive innovation research where people's social needs form the starting point for studies of how innovative solutions are developed in a way that contributes to real social change in the form of increased *empowerment* for individuals in combination with increased gender equality in organizations and society (cf. Cajaiba-Santana 2014; Dawson & Daniel 2010; Kabeer 2003; Lindberg & Berg Jansson 2016; Moulaert et al. 2005; Nussbaum 2011; Since 1999). The study shows that the organizations use empowerment within social innovation strategies in their operations. Among these strategies, *re-engagement* strategies are most common, where women's contributions and position are highlighted. The second most common strategy is *reformulation*, where women's access to resources is used as leverage in gender equality work. The least frequent strategy is the creation of new theories and definitions (*new visions*). Organizations could influence both micro and macro structures with normative work from the organizations. The strategies are used at all levels, even if *new visions* are created at the meso level to influence the macro level - e.g. with *the quadruple helix* - or influence the micro level through various creative meeting places for individuals. The overall picture that emerges is that organizations are working with *reformulation* at the macro level, with *new visions* at the meso level, and with *reintegration* at the micro level.

Prospects

To deepen knowledge about the possibilities and limitations of using the empowerment perspective for inclusive innovation, future studies would need to expand the understanding of the interplay between micro-, meso-, and macro-levels in such processes. This is because future studies can create connections between strategies and results, which is possible after some time, with a historical perspective. This study can be a valuable starting point for such studies. For example, it has been shown how the organizations studied, in the spirit of Phelps (2013), have created creative meeting places for a more inclusive understanding of the concept of innovation with a gender perspective on entrepreneurship and innovative activities. The main question is how people, organizations and society can together improve the conditions for promoting and developing socially innovative solutions.

Future research could investigate how an inclusive approach can contribute to a more innovative society and replace, for example, the strictly utility-maximizing ideal ("homo economicus") in the formation of economic systems and societies. An example of this renaissance is evident in the opening quotation of the study, by Phelps (2013), who argues that innovation is a way of living, thinking and acting. When people's needs are met and individuals absorb knowledge, art and music—and are encouraged to act and instigate change—additional value is generated in the form of an innovative, forward-looking society. An important lesson from Phelps is that an inclusive society helps increase the innovative activities of many different people. Phelps' insights highlight the value of developing the empowerment perspective to highlight and understand the processes of individual, organizational, and societal renewal pursued by the organizations studied. However, he believes that the large-scale nature of modern society, with decision-making processes that take place far from citizens and the economic dominance of large corporations and banks, has led to a dismantling of individual possibilities for action and a reduction in grassroots innovative activities.

Another aspect that needs to be explored is the organizations' endeavour to improve people's lives by increasing their opportunities to realize their innovative ideas within the framework of existing organizational and societal opportunities and limitations. This focus on increased *empowerment* (cf. Kabeer 2003; Nussbaum 2011; Sen 1999) show that social relations are permeated by power aspects such as status, resources, knowledge, etc. This needs to be considered by future research on the empowerment perspective in order to be able to distinguish and understand the mechanisms behind the development of future solutions in a more complex way than before. The activities of the organizations studied show that the masculine norms that have so far characterized innovation research limit the possibility of discovering women's innovations because they often develop in sectors, industries and forms that are rarely studied in the context of innovation (cf. Alsos and others 2013; Andersson et al. 2012; Lindberg 2012; Lindberg & Schiffbänker 2013; Pettersson 2007). Instead, the organizations are developing language and tools that can increase the opportunities to make women's innovation development visible and valued (cf. Foss 2009; Hill 2009; Nudd & Whalen 2009). This study shows that when organizations' activities are analysed from an empowerment perspective, their potential importance for the innovative development of individuals, organizations, and society becomes visible, which constitutes an important insight for future research.

Inspired by this study, the concept of empowerment can in the future be used to examine how gender equality in political strategies for innovative social development is often reduced to statistics, numbers and quantitative proportions of women and men. This study shows that more qualitative aspects of power must also be considered, to make visible and change both segregating and hierarchical gender patterns in organizations and society. As discussed above, in the case of the organizations, it is primarily about women's power over their own lives and the development of society in general through the opportunity to realize their ideas. The organizations attempt to achieve this bridging of quantitative and qualitative aspects by translating the social needs they have identified among the women they involve into proposed solutions aimed at politicians, civil servants and other decision-makers.

Future research on the empowerment perspective also needs to challenge the dominant technological perspective in innovation research and policy by highlighting the power aspects in how innovation is defined (cf. Alsos and others 2013; Andersson et al. 2012; Lindberg 2012; Lindberg & Schiffbänker 2013; Pettersson 2007). This study shows that the organizations studied do this by highlighting the importance of social innovations for the development of individuals, organizations and society. This means a reduction in prevailing gender patterns of segregation and hierarchy within the innovation field (cf. Lindberg & Berglund 2016; Lindberg et al. 2015) in accordance with the theoretical perspective *of undoing gender* (cf. Deutsch 2007; Lindberg & Schiffbänker 2013) since innovation development in a range of different forms, industries and sectors then becomes relevant to study in order to understand how innovative solutions to social needs and societal challenges are developed. Future research can take note of this.

Access to information, dissemination of information and education are important elements in the change of current institutions (cf. Mokyr 2009). Empowerment within social innovation can contribute to this by creating an understanding of how innovation development can be analyzed among a diversity of actors, areas and forms. As a *boundary object* or *quasi-concept* (cf. Lindberg & Portinson Hylander 2017; Star 1988), the empowerment perspective can serve as a starting point for a cross-border understanding of innovative development in many different forms and contexts where different local interpretations can be accommodated, just as this study shows that the organizations studied do.

References

Aagaard Nielsen Kurt & Svensson Lennart, red. (2006). *Action research and interactive research – beyond practice and theory.* Maastricht: Shaker Publishing.

Abrahamsson Lena (2000). *Att återställa ordningen - könsmönster och förändringarbetsorganisationer.* Umeå: Boréa.

Acker Joan (1999). "Gender and organizations". I Chafetz Saltzman Janet (red.). *Handbook of the Sociology of Gender.* New York: Kluwer Academic.

Alsos Gry Agnete, Ljunggren Elisabet & Hytti Ulla (2013). Gender and innovation – state of the art and a research agenda. *International Journal of Gender and Entreprenurship.* Vol. 5. Nr. 3. S. 236-256.

Amundsdotter Eva (2010). *Att framkalla och förändra ordningen – aktionsorienterad genusforskning för jämställda organisationer.* Doktorsavhandling. Luleå: Luleå tekniska universitet.

Andersson Eira (2012). *Malmens manliga mysterium – En interaktiv studie om kön och tradition i modernt gruvarbete.* Doktorsavhandling. Luleå: Luleå tekniska universitet.

Andersson Susanne, Berglund Karin, Gunnarsson Ewa & Sundin Elisabeth, red. (2012). *Promoting Innovation – Policies, Practices and Procedures.* Stockholm: VINNOVA.

Berglund Karin & Danilda Inger (2008). "Interaktiv kritisk forskning – En arena för omprövning av gemensam kunskap". I Johannisson Bengt, Gunnarsson Ewa & Stjernberg Torbjörn (red.). *Gemensamt kunskapande - den interaktiva forskningens praktik.* Växjö: Acta Wexionensia.

Berglund Knut-Erland, Lindberg Malin & Nahnfeldt Cecilia (2016). Social innovation now and then in the Church of Sweden. *Diaconia – Journal for the Study of Christian Social Practice.* Vol. 7. Nr. 2. S. 125-141.

Berglund Knut-Erland (2013). *Svenska storföretags Corporate Social Resonsibility-retorik - En studie av det kommunicerade företagsansvaret.* Licentiatuppsats. Uppsala: Uppsala Universitet.

Berglund Knut-Erland (2007). *The effect of microfinance on the empowerment of women and its societal consequences – A study of women self-help-group members in Andhra Pradesh.* Minor Field Studies-reports 2007:1. Uppsala: Uppsala Universitet.

Bohlin Henrik (2009). "Tyst kunskap ett mångtydigt begrepp". I Bornemark Jonna & Svenaeus Fredrik (red). *Vad är praktisk kunskap?* Stockholm: Södertörns högskola.

Bryman Alan (2002). *Samhällsvetenskapliga metoder.* Stockholm: Liber.

Cajaiba-Santana Giovany (2014). Social innovation: Moving the field forward. A conceptual framework. *Technological Forecasting & Social Change.*Vol 82. S. 42-51.

Carayannis Elias G & Campbell David FJ (2010). Triple Helix, Quadruple Helix and Quintuple Helix and how do knowledge, innovation and the environment relate to each other? A proposed framework for a transdisciplinary analysis of sustainable development and social ecology. *International Journal of Social Ecology and Sustainable Development.* Vol. 1. Nr. 1. S. 41–69.

Chalmers Alan F (2005). *What is this thing called science?* Milton Keynes: Open University Press.

Cipolla Carla, Melo Patricia & Manzini Ezio (2015) Collaborative Services in Informal Settlements: Social Innovation in Pacified Favela in Rio de Janeiro. I Nicholls Alex, Simon Julie & Gabriel Madeleine (Eds.) *New Frontiers in Social Innovation Research.* Palgrave Macmillan.

Coghlan David & Brydon-Miller Mary, red. (2014). *The SAGE Encyclopedia of Action Research.* London: SAGE.

Czarnaiwska Barbara & Sevon Gueje (2005). *Global Ideas: How ideas, objects and practices travel in the global economy.* Malmö: Liber.

Davis Karen (1999). "Närhet och gränsdragning – att nå andra sorters kunskap genom deltagande observation". I Sjöberg Katarina (red.). *Mer än kalla fakta - Kvalitativ forskning i praktiken.* Lund: Studentlitteratur.

Davies Anna & Simon Julie (2013). "Engaging Citizens in Social Innovation: A short guide to the research for policy makers and practitioners". 7th Framework Programme, Brussels: European Commission, DG Research

Dawson Patrick & Daniel Lisa (2010). Understanding social innovation: a provisional framework. *International Journal of Technology Management.* Vol. 51. Nr. 1. S. 9-21.

Deutsch Francine M (2007). 'Undoing Gender'. *Gender & Society.* Vol. 21 Nr. 1. S. 106-127.

Docherty Peter, Ljung Anders & Stjernberg Torbjörn (2008). "Interaktiv forskning – utveckling, användning och spridning av kunskaper". I Johannisson Bengt, Gunnarsson Ewa & Stjernberg Torbjörn (red.). *Gemensamt kunskapande: den interaktiva forskningens praktik*. Växjö: Acta Wexionensia.

Du Rietz Anita (2013). *Kvinnors entreprenörskap under 400 år*. Stockholm: Dialogos.

Eduards Maude (2002). *Förbjuden handling – om kvinnors organisering och feministisk teori*. Malmö: Liber.

European Commission (2013a). *Guide to social innovation*. Brussels: European Union.

European Commission (2013b). *Social innovation research in the European Union – Approches, findings and future directions*. Brussels: European Commission.

Evers Adalbert & Ewert Benjamin (2015). Social Innovation for Social Cohesion. I Nicholls Alex, Simon Julie & Gabriel Madeleine (Eds) *New Frontiers in Social Innovation Research*. Palgrave Macmillan.

Foss Sonja K. (2009). *Rhetorical Criticism: exploration and practice*. Waveland Press.

Furberg Mats (1981). *Verstehen och förstå - Funderingar kring ett tema hos Dilthey, Heidegger och Gadamer*. Karlshamn: Doxa.

Godin Benoit (2012). Social innovation: Utopias of Innovation from c. 1830 to the present. Working Paper No. 11. Project on the Intellectual History of Innovation. Montréal: Institut national de la recherché scientifique (INRS).

Gunnarsson Ewa & Westberg Hanna (2008). "Från ideal till verklighet – att kombinera ett könsperspektiv med en interaktiv ansats". I Johannisson Bengt, Gunnarsson Ewa & Stjernberg Torbjörn (red.). *Gemensamt kunskapande - den interaktiva forskningens praktik.* Växjö: Acta Wexionensia.

Gunnarsson Ewa & Westberg Hanna (2006). *Skelett i garderoben – Metoder för att upptäcka ojämställdhet.* Stockholm: Arbetslivsinstitutet.

Gunnarsson Ewa (2007). "The other sides of the coin – A feminist perspective on robustness in science and knowledge production". *International Journal of Action Research.* Vol 3. Nr 3. S. 349-363.

Habermas Jürgen (1996). *Kommunikativt handlande – Texter om språk, rationalitet och samhälle.* Göteborg: Daidalos.

Hakelius Johan (1995). *Den österrikiska skolan – Introduktion till humanistisk nationalekonomi.* Stockholm: Timbro.

Hansson Jens, Björk Fredrik, Lundborg David & Olofsson Lars-Erik (2014). *An Ecosystem for Social Innovation in Sweden – A strategic research and innovation agenda.* Lund: Lund University.

Herr Kathryn & Andersson Gary L. (2014) *The Action Research Dissertation - A guide for Students and Faculty.* (2 uppl). Los Angeles: Sage.

Hill Forbes I. (2009) "The 'Traditional' perspective". Kuypers Jim A. (Eds.) *Rhetorical Criticism: Perspectives in Action.* New York: Lexington Books.

Holmstrand Lars (2008). "Forskningscirklar – ett sätt att demokratisera kunskapsbildning?". I Johannisson Bengt,

Gunnarsson Ewa & Stjernberg Torbjörn (red.). *Gemensamt kunskapande: den interaktiva forskningens praktik*. Växjö: Acta Wexionensia.

Howaldt Jürgen, Kopp Ralf & Schwarz Michael (2015). Social Innovations as Drivers of Social Change – Exploring Tarde's Contribution to Social Innovation Theory Building. I Nicholls Alex, Simon Julie & Gabriel Madeleine (Eds.) *New Frontiers in Social Innovation Research*. Palgrave Macmillan.

Johannisson Bengt (2008). "Iscensättande forskning – om att kunskapa genom att initiera evenemang". I Johannisson Bengt, Gunnarsson Ewa & Stjernberg Torbjörn (red.). *Gemensamt kunskapande - den interaktiva forskningens praktik*. Växjö: Acta Wexionensia.

Johansson Anders W & Lindberg Malin (2011). Making a case for gender-inclusive innovation through the concept of creative imitation. *Annals of Innovation & Entrepreneurship*. Vol. 2. Nr. 2. Sid 1-13.

Johansson Anders W & Lindhult Erik (2008). Emancipation or workability? *Action research*. Vol 6. Nr 1. Sid 95-115.

Johansson Anders W (2008). "Kritisk reflektion och handling i interaktiv forskning". I Johannisson Bengt, Gunnarsson Ewa & Stjernberg Torbjörn (red.). *Gemensamt kunskapande - den interaktiva forskningens praktik*. Växjö: Acta Wexionensia.

Johnson Ross Freya & Goddard Ceri (2015). *Unequal Nation: The case for social innovation to work for a gender equal future*. London: The Young Foundation.

Jonsson Ivar (2014). "Quadro Helix Dynamics – from Social Innovation to Creative Communities – A Theoretical Framework". I Bernhard Iréne (red.). *Uddevalla Symposium 2014 - Geography of Growth The Frequency, Nature and Consequences of Entreprenurship and Innovation in Regions of Varying Density.* Reports 2014:2 University West.

Kabeer Naila (2003). *Discussing Women's empowerment – Theory and Practice.* Stockholm: SIDA.

Kvande Elin (2003). "Doing gender in organizations – theoretical possibilities and limitations". I Gunnarsson Ewa, Andersson Susanne & Vänje Rosell Annika (red.). *Where have all the structures gone? Doing gender in Organisations, Examples from Finland, Norway and Sweden.* Stockholm: Stockholm University.

Lindberg Malin & Hylander Portinson Jens (2017). Boundary dimensions of social innovation: Negotiating conflicts and compatibilities when developing a national agenda. *Innovation: The European Journal of Social Science Research.* Vol. 30. Nr 2. S. 168-181.

Lindberg Malin & Johansson Anders (2017). "Gender-sensitive Business Counselling – Changing Gendered Patterns and Understandings of Entrepreneurship". I Wynarczyk, Pooran & Ranga, Marina, *Technology, Commercialization and Gender: A Global Perspective.* London: Palgrave Macmillan.

Lindberg, Malin & Nahnfeldt Cecilia (2017). "Gendered Potentials and Delimitations in the Church of Sweden's Social Innovation". *Diaconia – Journal for the Study of Christian Social Practice.* Vol. 8. No 1. S. 3-22.

Lindberg, Malin & Berg Jansson, Anna (2016). Regional social innovation – pinpointing socially inclusive change for smart, inclusive and sustainable growth in European regional development policy. *International Journal of Innovation and Regional Development*. Vol. 7. Nr 2. S. 123-140.

Lindberg Malin & Berglund Knut-Erland (2016). "Gendered social innovation – a new research stream for gender inclusive innovation policy, research and practice". I Alsos Gry Agnete, Hytti Ulla & Ljunggren Elisabet (red.). *Research Handbook on Gender and Innovation*. Cheltenham: Edward Elgar Publishing.

Lindberg Malin, Forsberg Lena & Karlberg Helena (2016). Gender dimensions in women's networking for social innovation. Innovation: *The European Journal of Social Science Research*. Vol. 29. Nr. 4. S. 408-421.

Lindberg, Malin (2015a). Democratising Innovation Policy by Gender Scientific Participatory Research. I Gunnarsson, E., Hansen, H. P., Steen Nielsen, B. & Sriskandarajah, N. (red.). *Action Research for Democracy – New Ideas and Perspectives from Scandinavia*. New York: Routledge.

Lindberg, Malin (2015b). Women Resource Centres – a democratic innovation for gender equal growth?. I S. K. Sanders & Y. Gradskova (red.). *Institutionalizing Gender Equality – a Historical and Global Perspectives*. London: Lexington Books. S. 105-125.

Lindberg Malin, Forsberg Lena & Karlberg Helena (2015). Gendered social innovation – a theoretical lens for analysing structural transformation on organisations and society. *Int. J. Social Entrepreneurship and Innovation.* Vol. 3. Nr. 6. S. 472-483.

Lindberg, Malin (2014). "From exclusion to inclusion in public innovation support? Innovative practices in bottom-up networks". *Scandinavian Journal of Public Administration.* Vol. 18. Nr. 4. S. 91-107.

Lindberg Malin, Lindgren Monica & Packendorff Johann (2014). "Quadruple Helix as a Way to Bridge the Gender Gap in Entreprenurship – The Case of an Innovation System Project in the Baltic Sea Region." *Journal of the Knowledge Economy.* Vol. 5. Nr. 1. S. 94-113.

Lindberg, Malin & Schiffbänker, Helene (2013). Entry on gender and innovation. I Carayannis, E. G. (red.). *Encyclopedia of Creativity, Invention, Innovation and Entrepreneurship.* New York: Springer. S. 782-789.

Lindberg Malin (2012). A striking pattern – Co-construction of innovation, men and masculinity in Sweden's innovation policy. I Andersson, S., Berglund, K., Thorslund, J., Gunnarsson, E. & Sundin, E., (red.). *Promoting Innovation – Policies, Practices and Procedures.* Stockholm: VINNOVA. S. 47-67.

Lindberg Malin, Danilda, Inger & Torstensson, Britt-Marie (2012). Women Resource Centres – Creative Knowledge Environments of Quadruple Helix. *Journal of the Knowledge Economy.* Vol 3, Nr. 1. S. 36-52.

Lindberg Malin (2010). *Samverkansnätverk för innovation – En interaktiv och genusvetenskaplig utmaning av innovationspolitik och innovationsforskning.* Doktorsavhandling. Luleå: Luleå tekniska universitet.

Lindholm Gunilla (2002). "Kunskapsverkstad som redskap i fysisk planering". I Svensson Lennart, Brulin Göran, Ellström Per-Erik &

Widegren Örjan (red.). *Interaktiv forskning – för utveckling av teori och praktik*. Stockholm: Arbetslivsinstitutet.

Lindhult Erik (2008). "Att bedöma och uppnå kvalitet i interaktiv forskning". I Johannisson Bengt, Gunnarsson Ewa & Stjernberg Torbjörn (red.). *Gemensamt kunskapande – den interaktiva forskningens praktik*. Växjö: Acta Wexionensia.

Magnusson Lars (2002). *Sveriges ekonomiska historia*. Stockholm: Prisma.

McGowan Katharine & Westley Frances (2015) At the Root of Change: The History of Social Innovation. I Nicholls A. Simon J. & Gabriel M. (2015). *New Frontiers in Social Innovation Research*. New York: Palgrave Macmillan.

Merton Robert K. (2012). "On sociological theories of the middle range (1949)". I Calhoun Craig, Gerteis Joseph, Noody James, Pfaff Steven & Virk Indermohan (red.). *Classical Sociological Theory*. New York: Wiley-Blackwell.

Mokyr Joel (2009). *The Enlightened Economy – Britain and the Industrial Revolution 1700-1850*. London: Penguin Books.

Moulaert Frank, Martinelli Flavia, Swyngedouw Erik & Gonzalez Sara (2005). Towards Alternative Model(s) of Local Innovation. Vol. 42. Nr. 11. S. 1969-1990.

Mulgan Geoff, Tucker Simon, Ali Rushanara & Sanders Ben (2007). "Social Innovation - What it is, why it matters and how it can be accelerated". *Skoll Centre for social entreprenurship*. Oxford SBS.

Nahnfeldt Cecilia & Lindberg Malin (2013). *Är det nå'n innovation – Att nyttiggöra hum/sam forskning*. Karlstad: Karlstad University Press.

Nobelkommittén (2006). *The Nobel Peace Prize 2006. The official web site of the Nobel Foundation*. http://www.nobelprize.org. Hämtad 2006-10-24.

Nowotny Helga, Scott Peter & Gibbons Michael (2001). *Re-thinking Science –Knowledge and the Public in the age of Uncertanity*. Cambridge: Blackwell.

Nudd Donna M. & Whalen Kristina L. (2009). Feminist Analysis. I Kuypers Jim A. (Eds.) *Rhetorical Criticism: Perspectives in Action*. New York: Lexington Books.

Nussbaum Martha C. (2011). *Främja Förmågor – En modell för mänsklig utveckling*. Stockholm: Karneval Förlag.

Näringsdepartementet (2012). *Den nationella innovationsstrategin*. Stockholm: Näringsdepartementet.

Olsson Gudrun (2002). "Relationen mellan forskningen och praktik". I Svensson Lennart, Brulin Göran, Ellström Per-Erik & Widegren Örjan (red.). *Interaktiv forskning – för utveckling av teori och praktik*. Stockholm: Arbetslivsinstitutet.

Pettersson Katarina & Lindberg Malin (2013). "Paradoxical spaces of feminist resistance - mapping the margin to the masculinist innovation discourse. *International Journal of Gender and Entreprenurship*. Vol. 5. Nr. 3. S. 323-341.

Pettersson Katarina (2007). *Men and male as the norm? A gender perspective on innovation policies in Denmark, Finland and Sweden.* Stockholm: Nordregio.

Phelps Edmund (2013). *Mass Flourishing – How Grassroots Innovation Created Jobs, Challenge and Change.* Oxford: Princeton University Press.

Phelps Edmund (2007). *Macroeconomics for a modern Economy. The American Economic Review.* Vol. 97. Nr.3. S. 543-561.

Pol Eduardo & Ville Simon (2009). Social Innovation: Buzz word or enduring term? *The Journal of Socio-Economics.* Vol. 38. S. 878-885.

Ranga Marina and Etzkowitz Henry (2010). "Creative Reconstruction - A Triple Helix-based Innovation Strategy in Central and Eastern Europe Countries". I Mohammed Saad & Zawdie Girma (red.). *Theory and Practice of Triple Helix Model in Developing Countries, Issues and Challenges.* London: Routledge.

Schwartz Mark S & Carroll Archie (2003). "Corporate Social Responsibility – A three domain approach". *Business Ethics Quarterly.* Vol. 13. Nr. 4. S. 503-530.

Schwencke Eva (2006). "Free space in action research and in project-oriented traineeship". I Aagaard Nielsen Kurt & Svensson Lennart (red.). *Action research and interactive research – beyond practice and theory.* Maastricht: Shaker Publishing.

Sen Amartya (1999). *Development as Freedom.* New York: Oxford University Press.

Star Susan Leigh (1988). The structure of ill-structured solutions – Boundary objects and heterogeneous distributed problem solving. I

Huhns Michael & Gasser Les (red.). *Readings in distributed artificial Intelligence*. Kaufman, Menlo Park, CA. Stockholm: VINNOVA.

Svensson Lennart, Brulin Göran & Ellström Per-Erik (2002a). "Innovations- och lärprocesser i den nya ekonomin". I Svensson Lennart, Brulin Göran, Ellström Per-Erik & Widegren Örjan (red.). *Interaktiv forskning – för utveckling av teori och praktik*. Stockholm: Arbetslivsinstitutet.

Svensson Lennart, Brulin Göran, Ellström Per-Erik & Widegren Örjan, red. (2002b). *Interaktiv forskning – för utveckling av teori och praktik*. Stockholm: Arbetslivsinstitutet.

Tjornbo Ola (2015). Can Collective Intelligence Produce Social Innovation?. I Nicholls Alex, Simon Julie & Gabriel Madeleine (Eds.) *New Frontiers in Social Innovation Research*. Palgrave Macmillan.

Törnqvist Gunnar (2004). *Kreativitetens geografi*. Stockholm: SNS.

Urban Klas & Åmark Klas (2010). "Social Rights and Social Security: The Swedish Welfare State 1900-2000". Scandinavian Journal of History. Vol 26. Nr. 3. S. 157-176.

Van Oosterhout Hans J. & Heugens Pursey P.M.A.R. (2008). "Much Ado about Nothing: A Conceptual Critique of Corporate Social Responsibility" I Crane Andrew, McWilliams Abagail, Matten Dirk, Moon Jeremy och Siegel Donald S. (Eds.) *The Oxford Handbook of Corporate Social Responsibility*. Oxford University Press.

West Candance & Zimmermann Don H (1987). Doing gender. *Gender & Society*. Vol 1. Sid 125-151.

Wingblad Rune & Jonsson Seth (2008). "'Praktikdriven teori' – mot en nu interaktiv forskningsstrategi". I Johannisson Bengt,

Gunnarsson Ewa & Stjernberg Torbjörn (red.). *Gemensamt kunskapande – den interaktiva forskningens praktik.* "Växjö: Acta Wexionensia.

Winther Jörgensen Marianne (2008). "På framkant: interaktiv forskning och vetenskapens plats i samhället". I Johannisson Bengt, Gunnarsson Ewa & Stjernberg Torbjörn (red.). *Gemensamt kunskapande – den interaktiva forskningens praktik.* Växjö: Acta Wexionensia.

Zohir Sajjad & Matin Imran (2004). Wider impacts of Microfinance Institutions - Issues and Concepts. *Journal of International Development* Vol. 16. S. 301-330.